Behind The Black

To Yaroma

Detox.

May this be the first step
of many towards a world
filled with the Light.

(former patient)

Behind the Black

A Fearless Venture Into the Darkest Corners
of the Creative Mind In Search of Light

Colleen Black

foreword by Ana Weber

NEW YORK

Behind the Black
A Fearless Venture Into the Darkest Corners of the Creative Mind In Search of Light

Published in New York, New York, by Morgan James Publishing. Morgan James and The Entrepreneurial Publisher are trademarks of Morgan James, LLC. www.MorganJamesPublishing.com

The Morgan James Speakers Group can bring authors to your live event. For more information or to book an event visit The Morgan James Speakers Group at www.TheMorganJamesSpeakersGroup.com.

A free eBook edition is available with the purchase of this print book.

ISBN 9781630471866 paperback
ISBN 9781630471873 eBook
ISBN 9781630471880 hardcover
Library of Congress Control Number:
2014934767

CLEARLY PRINT YOUR NAME ABOVE IN UPPER CASE

Instructions to claim your free eBook edition:
1. Download the BitLit app for Android or iOS
2. Write your name in **UPPER CASE** on the line
3. Use the BitLit app to submit a photo
4. Download your eBook to any device

Cover Design by:
Rachel Lopez
www.r2cdesign.com

Interior Design by:
Chris Treccani
www.3dogdesign.net

In an effort to support local communities, raise awareness and funds, Morgan James Publishing donates a percentage of all book sales for the life of each book to Habitat for Humanity Peninsula and Greater Williamsburg.

Get involved today, visit
www.MorganJamesBuilds.com

Habitat
for Humanity®
Peninsula and
Greater Williamsburg
Building Partner

Behind the Black

Endorsements:

Written by: Colleen Black
Foreword by: Ana Weber
Edited by: Don Seeley

To the amazing women in my life who've provided me with more love and inspiration than all the ants in France doin' a monkey dance— my daughters Angela, Mikayla, and my god-daughter Deanna. Thank you for the light you add to my life in every moment. And to my mom who never once doubted me, even in the faces of fire breathing dragons.

Special thanks to Ana Weber, my remarkable friend, fellow author, and my inspiration to finish this book. Heartfelt appreciation goes out to my editor, Don Seeley, for doing such a wonderful job in fine-tuning my story.

Heartfelt gratitude also goes out to the marvelous men who have made such a difference in my life. You've been my heroes, my knights in shining armor and my lights in the darkness. Thank you for all your love and support Joe, Andy, and Tom, my amazing brothers. To my dad James Black for the strength and honor and love you have always provided. To my stepdad Joe for the best advice a daughter could ever wish for. And to all my grandparents for their lifetimes of wisdom. An especially LOUD belly laugh for the love and laughter from my adopted grandpa Wayne Elliot.

Behind the Black
Contents

by Ana Weber

Foreword

Presently I hold numerous careers; I coach entrepreneurs, professionals and students. I write books and I interview highly recognized people and I write blogs, I speak and I lecture, and I support various charitable organizations, I get to meet and connect with people from all walks of life, different cultures and from the various corners of the world; I feel lucky and blessed. I meet business owners, artists, entertainers, celebrities, highly recognized professionals, executives, students, inventors, authors and the list goes on and on. I embrace these connections one by one and I build relationships with people while I personally grow and learn to understand the importance of relationships and the wisdom we can extract from each and every one of them. I help others expose their shine and I love what I do. These relationships play a huge role in our lives and they contribute to our well-being, our personal happiness and motivate us to move on and move forward and in the process, recharge the energy and feel the strength and the courage to say good-bye to all yesterdays.

Meeting Colleen Black is an exceptional and intriguing story and I am thrilled and delighted to share it with you.

In July of 2013, my husband and I were sailing on the ship "Marina" with Oceania cruises thorough the Baltic Sea. This cruise was spectacular and above and beyond our expectations.

On a late afternoon, while we were getting ready for our first fine dining experience of an Italian meal on the ship, I tuned in to the on-board TV station to listen to the local announcements and weather information. Mr. Perez, the cruise director came on with his usual smile and with such enthusiasm announced the warm local weather and also made a few important announcements about the morning shore excursions. I was just about ready to turn off the TV when Mr. Perez briefly introduced Colleen Black's work on display on the ship; her spectacular sculptures and oil paintings followed by Colleen's appearance on the screen.

Watching Colleen's work, combined with her appearance hypnotized my entire being and I found myself drawn and deeply inspired. The vivid colors in her paintings, the shapes and the design of her sculptures spoke a trillion words.

That very moment, I felt intrigued and curious; who is Colleen Black? Where does she get this amazing talent? What are the feelings behind the art contributing to such beauty and color—not to mention the uniqueness and the finesse striking it all so powerfully?

I had to find out more about this lady. I knew right there and then that I wanted to try to connect with her and get to know her. I was eager to learn more about her work, her story, and all that lead her to this very moment filled with such extraordinary art.

We arrived back home on U.S. soil on the 18th of July, 2013 and a couple of days after recuperating from jet lag, I followed my intuition and pursuit to find and speak with Colleen.

At first I spoke to Colleen's agent. I gave him my contact information. Ten days later Colleen called me from Seattle; where she currently lives.

It was a profound moment; I felt like I had known her all my life and the energy between us was fantastic. Colleen and I connected fabulously over the telephone and after numerous telephone conversations talking about life, family, friends, experiences and work, I asked Colleen the following question: "Would you consider writing a book about your life, your feelings and the emotions behind each and every piece you create? Tell the story, Colleen, so people from all over the world will embrace your art and get to understand it and love it just like you do and experience and feel with you all that is behind the work."

Colleen listened intently and a week later, she began writing and she couldn't stop; there was a magical flow and as she was sharing with me chapter after new chapter, I've come to realize that she is not only an artist on canvas or clay, she is a true gifted writer as well. Colleen pours her entire being into her art; feelings, emotions, experiences, love, faith, energy, time; simply all that a human being possesses. It is all connected and at the same time, stands alone powerfully individually and exclusively. She writes as beautifully and intensely as she paints and does her sculptures. It is all so striking and amazing. Her creations are complete; the connection and the release between the artist and the work find a place in people's homes and people's hearts; a perfect link; illusion and reality; the yin and the yang in our lives we cannot consciously escape.

Colleen completed her book and her book *"Behind the Black"* speaks a trillion words of art. I am moved deeply and I can promise you that it will move you too. This book is a true beacon of light shining from far away, just like a lighthouse giving us signals we can trust and follow. More so, the book brings out our vulnerability, our feelings and emotions—understanding that we want to be free, express, share and give as much as we can throughout our personal journey and enjoy each and every moment of the gift in the present. Colleen's book gives you so much depth and clarity to understand your own personal challenges, changes and circumstances. Personally I feel that the book made me understand myself better, to be less judgmental and appreciate and like not only who I am, but how I am, and ultimately embrace life like never before.

"As we cross bridges, leading us to the next destination we can color the way and choose to paint it with our feelings."

Ana Weber: Life Coach-Speaker-Journalist-Blogger
Author: *360° of Success: Money – Relationships – Energy – Time*
The 4 Essential Ingredients to Create Personal and Professional Success
Winner of the "Business: Motivational" book category - 2013 USA Best
Book Awards
"*The Money Flow*" Radio Host healthylife.net

Behind the Black
Prologue

At the tender age of ten years old I was living inside a wonderland. The rolling green hills of Massillon, Ohio were my playground and every morning I seemed to wake up inside the life of a princess. I'd found my love in life inside the glorious world of art. I was a painter. My mom and dad were excited to see me so happily wrapped into this new found talent and all my friends and family shared their support. I have been lucky enough to be surrounded by this support my entire life. Concerns only came when people found out how much money I made, and rightfully so. But for the most part, besides the occasional stranger spouting into revolt only because of misinterpretation, I feel extremely blessed by every person I have met along the way and even more so to call them my friends and family.

I have the utmost respect and my heart swims in an overflowing pool of gratitude for every single one of them, because they all played a part in who I am today. But I owe a special thank you to my grandma Alice. Alice gave my wonderland a name. When showing her one of my paintings many years ago, she pointed to my full signature in the corner and said, "You know, you should sign your work C. Black. A lot of artists shorten their name like that."

Well, that was plenty of explanation for me. I was enamored by the fairytale life of an artist. But fairy tales have a dark side. It is this side of the story that makes every story great and gives art its depth. It makes the crescendos in life's symphonies roar across the landscape—bowling over every soul in its path, leaving us touched in the very darkest corners of our hearts—wanting to scream our bleak existences into the starry, starry nights with explanations of color and light and sweet, delicious poetry.

We are all a piece of this creation and every one of us relates to the fairy tales because of this beautiful human connection. We are each made special. Without certain instruments, a symphony could not create the rolling thunder, nor the snares play the pelting rain.

That beautiful day on the green grass with my grandma was transformative. Held in its hand was a destiny of a fate not yet realized. As time went on, the catharsis of art and the irony of having a last name like Black, would cause light to shine on every bleak little corner it could possibly reach, revealing new awareness of discovery, and the intense power of love to illuminate the storms that were lying ahead in my not so distant future.

References started to pool together as if my name were a purpose inside itself and I was ultimately destined to write the very book you hold so tenderly in your hands. Unfolding the story pages of life, answers rushed in and I was blown to pieces—a crystal explosion into an infinite sea of light and color. Lost inside a world I longed to be, instead I was left to wrap those iridescent fragments into a dark blanket of a reality I could not escape, this wrapping of skin and flesh and bone. Only through the fabric of canvas, the deep pores of clay, or the pages of writing was this inner light allowed to shine through like the twinkling stars of deep space. Although this is only a brief, infinitesimal glimpse at a world of possibility open to every last one of us, I feel it is and always has been my destiny to share it. There is no way to humanly describe the things that I have experienced or the light I have "seen" (sight is like a hindrance in this world, to REALLY see you have to look through the "eyes" of the heart). My hope is that you will experience what I have experienced someday. I truly hope ALL of us do. I sincerely hope that someday we all will see—beyond the black.

My first lesson on the depth of color itself came in a painting class I was in. My teacher, Jack Richard, explained that the deepest color of black comes from mixing all of the darkest colors together on a pallet. Although what we see and the neurons that connect this sight to make the colors we call "black" can vary, the depth is only reached by seeing of ALL the colors at once. The reason for this is that our amazing minds pick up on every tiny swirl of color that goes into a mixed black. It excites us. It excites the brain. A factory-made blended version may look the same and may even have the same color background... but for some reason the touch of anima or human soul exists deep within the regions of the swirls and I believe our HEARTS see THIS. This beautiful blending of all color can be compared to so much of life... so many circumstances. Inside the depths of our awareness there is a mix of everything that has brought us to where we are and inside this glory is where we can find treasures.

In the visible spectrum, white reflects light and is a presence of all colors, but black absorbs light and is an absence of color. This is exactly the opposite of what I just described when black is mixed as a pigment. It is also complementary and creates a symbiotic relationship between the two. Black sucks in all the rainbows and vacuums up every last little particle of light. It holds them tightly inside a swirling array of color that excites the eyes with depth and spurs the curious into its lair where all the secrets of the universe combine and dance off into the far reaches of infinity. Perhaps somewhere deep within the black holes of the universe all of this swirling color and light implodes to explode into a new dimension of ever expanding creativity in space and time.

Black is not usually a color associated with insight. Although it was the first color to be used by artists in Neolithic cave painting, it has often been associated with darkness and "scary" things. I guess I could have taken it face value and allowed my life to be painted full of "Halloweenish" scenes, but it was not meant to be. A light unexpectedly showed up and changed my destiny. To my advantage black goes with anything, which would explain my ability to pass the rigorous delegations of high school cliques with flying colors. Ancient Egyptians took the positive route and associated the color black or the color of "Anubis", god of the underworld, who took the form of a black jackal. The color black was protection against evil in the burial grounds of the dead. In the hierarchy of ancient Rome, while royalty wore purple, soldiers and officers adorned themselves in red and priests were allotted the pure and pristine color of white, artists were given robes of black. The color black has a rich history on the pages of the arts throughout the centuries. There are several musical references to the depth of this word, but my favorite one to listen to when I felt the rush, the surge of overpowering yet another of life's hurdles was "Back in Black" by AC/DC.

My hope is that as you read the stories throughout this book you are inspired to look a little deeper and open your sights more to the sweet possibilities of the roads that lie ahead and reflect kindly and gently to the worn paths that make up your past.

This is a true autobiography, meaning all the stories are written to the best of my recollection. You will have your own beliefs and opinions on certain matters throughout the book. I have the utmost respect for these and I truly hope that nothing comes across offensively. I suggest an open mind. I wrote it with one. I have grown up with my own names for things, as well as making up a few of my own descriptive words… my own Blacjectives, although I don't think they'll be adding any of them to Merriam Webster's lexicon anytime soon.

Thank you, most of all, for taking time to stop and read this book. The best of intentions lies between its pages with the hopes that your life is touched in a positive and uplifting way.

Chapter 1
DRAGON'S BREATH

I am so grateful just to have the breath to write this sentence. Whatever happens next is cake. The most beautiful things happen when we aren't looking, when we don't plan, when we have no agenda or set rules. Inside this space that I love so deeply and that many of us strive for, yearn for, and experience all too far and few between is where the creative light lives. This is where the pool of love begins and where we never die. It is the world of possibility and the joy in hope. It is everything we have never done but yearn for with our every fiber. It is an understanding of the deepest core of life and knowledge of nothing.

It pours through my fingers with a rush more powerful than Niagara Falls when I don't expect it and only if I am listening. When my mind is too busy telling the stories of what I think should happen… this place, this being or this space only listens. When I take the reins of life and create what I think it should be, it comes out the way it always has – falling short of my ambition, and somehow disappointingly dies in translation. But the moment I let go and open my heart and humbly bow my head, an awesome power that yearns to speak through me lights up the canvas or grabs hold of my clay and I can't help the joy and emotional bliss I feel as I watch an ethereal message from inside unfold in my art. It is a message of hope and inspiration inside the innocent dreams of a little girl who longed to live the life of a princess but was eaten by a dragon instead. The sun would kiss the corners of my eyes and trickle through my veins all the way to my toes in the mornings, sending me so much excitement and joy for my day that I would literally bounce from my bed in the waking moments of those warm summer days in Ohio. To have that same love for life now humbles me to no end.

In this mode, passion overtakes and consumes me and rides a beautiful wave. I have no power over this and I don't want it.

I never expected the life I was dealt. When asked if there are parts I would relive differently, I suppose that would make me a different human being and I do like what I have become, but the idea of different possibilities of me intrigues me if anything. Like any creative mind, I love to wander in and out of different worlds, and experience the opposite side of the coin. And I know now that the side was a choice, not a flip. This was written with an open understanding of this. If we are given the gift of the first morning light, we have the opportunity to create beauty, give life and share inspiration. These are pieces of heaven. There is also a hell. There IS such a thing as dragons. Monsters DO exist. I have been pulled from the jaws of many of them.

The Battle Inside

Here I sit awaiting something unknown
A future to which may be spent alone
A puddle of tears surrounds my fate,
As I sit observing I only await.
Death? Will I drown?
To this face I can only frown.
For a past open to me and unknown to others
Haunts my present and breaks my cover.

This face I put on is not my own
For deep down inside I've barely grown.
The little girl they once all knew,
Yah, she's still there, "sweet as morning dew".
But a painful fate awaits her love
And the once white feathers are turning to a black dove.
What can stop this eerie death rhyme?
The clock is ticking and so flows time.
Rhythm flows and no one knows
As her stomach ties in turbulent bows.
How can she stop this terrible end?
For there it is just around the bend.
Closer and closer the serpent creeps
As she stands upon a cliff so steep.
What can she do, where can she turn?
Closer to the fire she feels the burn.
And now surrounds her, the sting of pain.
And the beast has won once again.
The pain is great but does not kill,
The little girl inside me lives ... still.
But another battle to fight will soon arrive,
One only knows if she will survive.
Next time will the beast win or lose?
It's up to her, what will she choose?
For the day awaits and soon will come
When she and the beast will finally become one...

I was sixteen when I wrote that. I was sprawled out on the hardwood floors of my bedroom with nothing but a notebook to analyze the burning sensation of the dragon's breath. The beat of his heart consumed me; it's pulse steady and complete. I was helplessly falling through the threshold of the beast's lair. I stood outside of myself and looked back on something that had not happened yet and as the words poured out through my tears onto the paper I knew this tumultuous love affair had become some sweet black corner of my soul. Tucked away in a dark crevice, an empty bottle of cheap wine crept into the corner of my eye through the cracked open door of my closet. Although I was stone cold sober, the battle inside had exhausted me.

I remember my first drink like a child remembers their first time riding a bike. We were made for each other. It was a love affair with a beast that I knew... long before I ever ended up where I am now.

I was forty when I wrote this: "The first step in any twelve step program is to admit to yourself a powerlessness over the addiction. You cannot come to a place of healing with an ego. This first step is not taken in weakness but in utter and unadulterated strength."

It took a long time for enough humility to sink in for me to admit that the beast had won this battle. Even as I wrote this, it was as if a symphony and a stage filled with dancers seemed to come to a screeching halt inside my mind – set off by the twang of a broken string.

To admit that I am powerless over alcohol because it steals my soul takes guts. This is the only way that I have found to turn this beast filled with fire and glory, beauty and passion, into the despicable toothless troll that it truly is. All smoke and mirrors shatter and disappear into the vacuum of truth and this hairless vile little creature runs away whimpering...and waiting.

Inside its days of glory, it had the power to take away everything I truly loved. With the stealth of a lion, it hides patiently camouflaged in the tall brown grassy embers of my mind haunting my very existence. Every once in a while I catch a whiff of its scent and as the hairs rise on the back of my neck, I remember the powerful force that can kill me dead with the graceful slice of one claw.

There is a tantalizing dance whispering through the wind of memories that this looming creature of death sings like a siren calling to her sailor. In a single flutter of weakness there is nothing where there was everything and everything where there was nothing.

Simply forgetting that I drank and blanketing over the stealthy beast is not an option. It bites. Even smacking it with some self-righteous years of sobriety under my belt leaving it toothless and frail will not stop it. It has shark like powers to restore its powerful jaws and it just waits— swimming attentive circles in an ocean of its own drool to devour every last breath of beauty that blissfully dances inside the innocent child of my soul.

I don't like to pretend to have it all together. Over the years and the countless searches, one simple fact remains standing in the cinders of the war-stricken landscape of my soul. The truth certainly does set you free. Yet, should I forget this, my dark beastly friend is patiently waiting drooling over the taste of every pulsating rush of ego that trickles through my veins. If I forget for even a second that I am powerless over this beast, its voice is the cool calm whisper in the wind that lies to me about how it can make everything all better.

And should it sneak a taste past the guards, its sweet kiss of decadence licks my lips. It pretends to be where my fun always was and always will be. It even tricks my eyes into believing that the rest of the world is fully capable of having control and can enjoy life much more in its presence. This makes me think that I can too. After all it's only fair.

The beast has every one of my senses finely tuned to accept its lies. Even its smell can trigger my memory in a delicious way. I remember the cool refreshing burn as it rushes down past my taste buds through the vomit pool that almost passes the point of no return. The warmth seems to spiral into every nerve-ending, creating an exciting thunderstorm of power and lightning that sparks up my confidence. This is all happening within seconds of the first sip of alcohol and in milliseconds the second drink is needed to fill a burning itching desire that seems to have replaced everything else that matters. The world can fade to black as far as I'm concerned at this point, as long as I get that next drink.

It all becomes a blur and until I comfortably have the third and maybe even the fourth drink in my other hand, I will not be the least bit comfortable in my own skin. The obsession continues and now I must make sure that there is enough alcohol to kill a full-grown bull at my disposal. This obsession can go to the extent of securing my own stash in my purse or some hidden corner of a bathroom. Perhaps there is a person willing to buy my drinks with bottomless pockets, anything it takes.

Once I have established a plethora of alcohol, I can finally "relax" and enjoy the buzz. By this time the room is just starting to feel much warmer, welcoming and happy. ALL people look pretty and I have so much wit that even my slurs, stumbles, and the permanent grin or "permagrin" I wear across my face are HIGHLY attractive to all those around me. Or so it seems.

I am also in complete control, on top of the world, and have a very strong handle on philosophy and finely-tuned conversation. A rush of joy smacks me upside the back of the head every time I find one of those drinks that I have so cunningly hidden beneath the dessert table just in case the full bar should happen to run out. My confidence is through the roof, and looking across the room that gallery owner that I think is so aloof looks like a great target for a speech on humility. Another shot gives me the extra poise I need, and ...oops...hiccup....someone should fix the damn wrinkles in that carpet that are keeping me from a slightly less than perfect gate over to my fine unsuspecting target. I can figure out which one of him to talk to when I get there, of course...

The next morning, somehow my eyes seem to be a separate entity as the lids roll back like creaky garage doors to painfully reveal the light. There is a completely new room in my house... I try to focus, and my head reminds me of the first drink and maybe the second but fails to recall anything further. Complete remorse fills every corner of my mind as I realize there is a human lump breathing beside me in this strange room. Immediately the fight or flight instinct kicks in and I quietly look for my clothes and a way out. The throbbing sensation in my head is occasionally interrupted by really bad moments of clarity from the previous evening and my only prayer is to find my keys. If I am lucky I'll find my car. Did I drive? Thank God for GPS, at least I can track where I am. Trying not to wake the lump, I slither to the door, somehow manage to find my car after setting off the alarm a few times to remind me of exactly where it is. Pieces of memory keep panging into the corners of my mind and don't paint a pretty picture at all. I sit in the early morning traffic feeling so incredibly bad because the little pangs have become large bombs going off in my mind. I just want to forget.....and wait, o glorious joy… right there, before my bloodshot eyes, my aching heart, my tangled smelly mess of a human shell, right there is the LIQUOR STORE!!!

My soul has emptied; my human shell has taken on a new resident. Its name is alcohol and it has no regard for the beauty that once occupied its space. If she makes it back, she will be lucky. Every once in a while a tear will interrupt the lie that the alcohol has replaced my true form. My soul cries to return, but alcohol can shout louder, and it promises to let my TRUE feelings out. Its promises are all that are real to me in this world of darkness.

Someday I will find true love, someday I will be appreciated for who I truly am and I need a drink to help me to find this. Someday I will die, someday this will kill me… I need a drink to deal with that. Someday my two beautiful daughters could be taken from this fog I live in. Maybe that would be best, damn need a drink. I don't want to cry anymore… can anyone hear me? Does anyone care….? I'm all alone. There is nothing inside this darkness. The world would be much better off without me. I neeeeed a drink.

Yes, I am powerless over alcohol. It's been 4 months since my last drink. Writing this has been a real reminder of this. Life does come back. My soul is very tenderly making its way to the surface again. She's been beaten, held back, abused and ignored. A humble tear empathizes with the pain. I feed her daily with a prayer, fill her with the beautiful colors of God's great creation that seem to get brighter every moment, and tenderly coerce her into the things I once loved to do with my beautiful soul.

I swallowed the Dragon. The beast and I are one. Every morning for the rest of my life I wake up with dragon breath. No amount of mouthwash will take it away...and in fact some kinds of mouthwash feed it. Been there, drank that. Life is full of dragons of all shapes and sizes. They can fill our lives with darkness and gloom in the aftermath of their smoke-filled breath.

I wrote this book to perhaps provide a glimpse of the sparkles that lie deep within the ashes on the tiny bits of charcoal in a dragon's breath. I'm here to tell you that there is light in darkness and that you only need to see behind the black corners of life's troubles to find your own light.

Chapter 2
THE LITTLE GIRL

Deep within all of us there is always a kid. No matter how much growing up I've had to do, no matter what level of hell I've put myself through, one small thought can send the kid in me spinning through the ashes like a fairy wisping through fairy dust and into absolute love of creative adventure.

In the months that followed the aftermath of destruction I was leaving behind at age 40, I began to nurture and nurse the kid in me back into my life. Excitement filled me once more as I laid color to canvas, filled my fingers with clay, and let myself put pen to paper. She was shy, afraid and tender-seared raw by the abuse of the Dragon's breath. The empty promises that alcohol made remained just around every corner, and my soul heard them... and to this day continues to fear them. It is a slow steady process that continues to confront me with each new challenge. I'd dearly missed the child within and never want to see her return to the darkness. Next time she may not come back.

My life lies here, on this fragile thread called alcoholism. One day at a time, sometimes by the moment, I continue to experience the light; always aware of the looming cold dark places never far away.

I wrote this as I entered into a new existence. Even now, having years of sobriety under my belt does not make this reminder of the power of addiction any less overwhelming.

I cannot create anything worth saving while drinking. I tried. It was always fun in the moment. But the next day what once was stricken with shear genius turned into a, "What the **** was I thinking?"

I've ruined works of art by delving into them while drunk. So in the last years and through some of the harshest moments of my addiction, I had finally given up. It was in this final hour of solitude that I experienced a horror so deep and so real that it snapped me back from the grips of death itself.

I had been drinking almost a half-gallon of vodka every night and hid it in the dark moldy basement of the last house that I lived at in Pittsburgh. Over the past year I'd lost a lot. I was below the poverty level and only living in that house because a very close friend was kind enough to let us stay in the home she was losing to foreclosure. I had offered to live there and promised to pay rent only after I had used up my last "get out of having to pay rent for free" card at the artists co-op that I'd lived so happily in for the previous 11 years.

Things do not get better when you continue to drink and soon I was running so far behind in the rent that I was embarrassed to relay the empty promises to pay her. Somehow she understood though, and to this day, even the mention of her name fills me with warmth in knowing such kindness exists.

There was a roof over our heads, and in this I felt some semblance of hope for me and my two girls, but every dream seemed to be caving in and I could feel the cold winds of desperation creeping up and begging for answers. My electricity had been turned off for a few weeks and the only reason we were able to eat the last of the food in the refrigerator was because of a kind-hearted neighbor who noticed the darkness and hooked an extension cord to our house when he found out.

It was in the midst of these dark, desolate hours in my life that I finally made a decision to ask for help. I had hit rock-bottom and what I saw was a gaping, ferocious, never-ending pit of despair. To this day, I am grateful beyond tears that I did not fall any further.

I have heard many stories of hopeless bottoms that had to be experienced in order for the wakeup call to sink in completely. It is different for everyone. I suppose there are the supernatural wonders out there that simply take the advice they are given and never have to go through anything tough. As a mom, I can't help but wish this for my kids. I'm sure my parents had this wish for me as well. Knowing that I made it through is no consolation. I still hope that my girls will learn my life-lesson by osmosis.

There is a good side and a bad side to pushing boundaries. I feel extremely grateful to have made it to the positive side of this one.

It was a typical drunk evening, but one I will remember forever because it scared the bejeebers out of me. Even having been through so many pitfalls, I had never experienced anything even remotely close to that one fateful night. I had made it through bottoms that were absolute bottoms for other people, and ones that in sober moments, I had patted myself on the back for never having had to go through-nightmares, voices from dark corners of rooms that screamed my name in frightening and what should have been sobering wake-up calls. Just the thought of those bleak and frightening moments even now sends chills through my bones. This moment in my life was different, this one is the brick wall that I can pinpoint as the one where I lost my cape. I was no longer invincible. I was not afraid to die until this moment.

I now know that there is another form of death.

I was in my kitchen. I had broken down in tears once again. Thoughts of suicide disguised themselves as false hopes of relief. I had convinced myself once more that I was of no use any longer, and that I was not worth the breath I was breathing. Suddenly a cold chill surrounded and permeated my being. I smelled death. And as I looked up in the drunken state that I was in, all that I could see was the deepest darkest black that I have ever seen. It went beyond explanation and it was full of nothingness. It is what can be imagined as the darkest pit of lonely.

In that singular moment, I felt my soul leaving me. She seemed to turn and sadly wave goodbye with her head bent down, but her eyes filled with tears and stared right through me... she was giving up. It was not a near death experience. More like a threat of divorce. My sweet creative artist side was through, finished. She was going to leave and in this instant, I knew that I would die without her. Nothing like the death that I had felt would be a passage. A deeper than the darkest dark of fears entered a room in my mind and it left a black hole as a reminder. This sobering moment of realization remains the closest I ever want to come to the entrance to hell.

I had finally had enough. After years of hiding this from my family, I called my mom and admitted that I had been back on the juice and had come to the conclusion that there was no way out. This was when she decided to rescue me. She told me that she was coming to Pittsburgh and taking me and the girls with her. I packed my things over the next few months and sobered up for the plane ride home. My brothers came from across the country and drove my things home in a moving truck they had rented.

I'm very grateful for this. My entire family pitched in and literally pulled me from the jaws of death. My mom, my dad and my brothers all played a part in a drama I never wanted to create. I knew I had an amazing family, but I had never expected their unconditional love and support.

The hardest thing to do sometimes is to fall down on your knees, admit your futility and ask for help. I had been digging and scratching for sober survival for so long without success. I felt ashamed. Yet when I was well enough to turn it around in my mind, I realized that I would not hesitate for a single moment to do the same for them. In this, I gained understanding, respect and a very deep love for every part they played in reaching out.

Slowly, but surely, I nurtured my way back. I know now that I never again want the little girl inside of me to feel unwelcomed. But through this experience, I caught a whole new reflection of her. I didn't write the following little story in any of the above circumstances, in fact it was written years before this incident, but it seems to fit just right in this particular part of the bigger picture.

The Little Girl

Once upon a time there was a little girl. The little girl grew and as she grew, she came across bigger and bigger things. When her journey first began, everything seemed big. But as life swept her into its arms the things she experienced along the way took on different forms. The big scary things taunted her until she learned to taunt back. The heavy loads burdened her. She grew stronger with each new load and soon she could handle much more than those that came before. She learned not to look at any of the things as too scary or too heavy. She simply sighed and took what she'd been dealt and with each sigh there was a new air that entered her breath—a peace that overrode the pain of the experiences. Although she still cried, she still bled, and she still longed for the easy way around the big life she so steadily held.... she still grew.

One day the little girl came across something so big, so heavy...so scary that even with all the experience she'd been through, she stood before the thing that life had put in her path and wept. She wept for days and soon days turned to weeks. Time left her, and her tears enveloped her. It was a sadness she'd never experienced, a deep longing for what she did not know. She wanted to turn and run, leaving life for all the pain it had caused her. But as she turned, she saw the path she had taken. It had started as such a wide and worn path, one that so many had walked.

As life gave her the choices that it so often will, she saw the times that she'd taken, the harder less-traveled path ... and she remembered. Those paths were filled with all the great joys in life that she treasured. The paths had lessened and grown so small...but were filled with so much more. No one had taken the flowers along the way. No one had trampled the fresh green grass. And the hidden treasures were still hidden for her to find.

So she turned once more with a sigh. And the sigh gave her the breath. And the breath gave her peace. The little girl looked down to face what life had given her. There in her pool of tears was the thing that had seemed so scary, so big, and so heavy. She smiled, for it was now a thing of beauty.

And the reflection of a woman smiled back.

Chapter 3
THE SCIENCE OF ADDICTION

Inside sobriety there is a cool crispness to the clarity that slowly begins to clear away the cobwebs. It seems otherworldly after being smothered by darkness for any length of time. Mixed with natural curiosity and drive, clear thinking becomes a rocket ship into other dimensions. The answer, "just because" never made me sit still. I wanted to know why and how and fully understand the entirety of every nuance that made up a conclusion. No matter what the ingredients were, I wanted to know what made up the soup. In this way, life could be viewed from so many more angles, allowing me to paint new pictures the way I saw things and happily come to my own conclusions to the question, "What if?"

I once felt a really hard ball-shaped pain in my chest while I was taking a shower. The thought of any kind of cancer scared me so much that I stayed up all night researching every possibility. As a consequence, I learned that it was probably a cyst from drinking the loads of caffeine found in the energy drinks I was replacing with water. I also found a lot of articles on raw food diets that were linked with curing cancer. There was a green drink in particular that I latched onto and after a 10 day juice fast and the raw food diet that followed, by the time I made it to my mammogram appointment a month later the lump was nowhere to be found.

With all the information available on the Internet at our fingertips, each and every one of us is fully capable of seeing every situation from a bird's-eye view. That said, there are plenty of quacks to disrupt the symphonic sound wave of information that flows like the sweet tweets of little songbirds. Always have proper discernment when coming to your conclusions and ask trusted and certified professionals before any serious risks are taken.

"Ugly ducklings" can turn into swans, but it would have been a much easier migration into change had the signet known its true nature. Simply being called a name was not an answer for me—I had to know what made me an alcoholic. So into the pond of information I waddled, hoping to sift out the truth about addiction.

I'm not sure how research works for everyone, but it's pure ecstasy for me. With the first bit of new information striking like me like lightening, excitement rolls through me like a gigantic thunderstorm in the crackling heat of an afternoon in the desert. Each new spark of the unknown fractures a gap into a doorway that soon allows for sprinkles of light to creep into the shadows. Light spreads. Like showering blasts of pouring rain, it bounces off of everything and lights up the corners. They may seem dark… but with enough focus, mysteries begin to unravel. I find this to be true with discoveries and new information. Bouncing like liquid raindrops of light, every thread of information leads me on a journey through the unknown, casting just enough discovery into the shadows to draw me in, and take me further.

If I was to live with this beast called alcoholism, I wanted to know its background….where it grew up, who its friends were, and most of all its subtle weaknesses.

Much of my information stemmed from seeing the movie, "What the Bleep Do We Know!?." Seeing that movie was the sliver of light in the doorway that shed revelation on a path to new discoveries about how addictions of all forms work. There is a funny cartoon illustration in that film that gave my imagination some wonderful eye candy to further contemplate.

On a cellular level in our addictive state, we create receptors for the drug in need at a rate that is out of control. The best way for my mind to wrap itself around the concept was to imagine a bunch of little hungry Pacman-looking mouths spread across the surface of my cells. In active addiction, these receptors are young, vibrant and overstuffed with food, giving them reason to procreate in abnormal rates and covering our once healthy and balanced cells with an unbalanced amount of hungry little mouths. All screaming for one thing... MORE. Each receptor is built to accept one type of polypeptide...one protein made by the hypothalamus normally needed to create an emotional reaction. However, when addiction rages out of control these hungry little mouths rule the roost and can take control over what a cell "hungers" for.

To my understanding, these receptors do not die once we stop feeding them. They simply lie dormant. One drink, one tiny lump of sugar, or one more excuse to let anger control the situation is all that it takes to awaken an entire clan of hungry receptors. The screams are felt across every cell, and the obsession for another fix is overwhelming. The only way I am able to think myself through handling this is to replay through the whole story. Hangover and all.

All forms of addiction have horror stories. The terrible memories of the past can stand as soldiers in the present to ward off the onset of more of them. Every consequence of history past has to boldly step up bare-faced to the front line and engage in a full-on war to back the obsession back into the dark shadows that it occupies. For me, just a sip of alcohol is way too risky, so I must remember the destructive path it lead me to and resist it like the plague. Addiction is cunning. It will have you remembering only the happy parts. A monster of deception lives in that space. Never let the candy-coated cottage in the woods fool you. That monster will eat you alive.

Puppet

Like a marionette controlled by invisible strings, dancing with an addiction can become a dance lost in the confusion of just who has the control.

In my attempts to understand this lack of control, I turned to my art. Inside the very act of creation I often find answers to questions that go beyond my understanding. Art speaks to me in the language of emotion. This is the most widely understood language while being extremely hard to translate at the same time. An entire chapter can be written on just one glance. This language of the heart communicates more quickly and succinctly than any form of communication. Captured in art this language of soul unites us in a common understanding of sheer truth.

A lump of clay soon took on the posture of a puppet hanging from strings. I cannot count the number of times I have collapsed in complete defeat. I've been lost in that desperation, feeling lifeless and drained. As the clay took on this emotion, I found myself wanting to place blame somewhere. Who had the strings? Was it alcohol? Or the harsh circumstances in life? … Maybe it was some grand puppeteer in the sky that took hold of me and made me do it…

Placing blame is an act of fear dressed in its best tuxedo serving a five star meal on a silver platter to our egos. I had to turn and face the origin of strings. The lifeless puppet in clay turned her head to face what she had created. Her fingers and toes curled into a position of awakening strength.

She was a puppet to an unseen puppeteer that she was creating inside her own dance. I'd seen some beautiful dances performed with ribbons and watched the ribbons themselves dance with the wind under complete control of the dancer's movement and this became an analogy that began to unravel the mystery that haunted me. I wished so badly to be free of the strings that held me and which seemed to have this control over me, but they'd become an inseparable part of me. I had lost the power to let go and the ribbons of addiction molded to my wrists and ankles. As they twisted through the air I sculpted them into fingers that became the hand of a giant. One that once seemed so monstrous, I now saw as an illusion. The middle finger is purposely attached to the curly locks of hair that blanket the corners of my mind. After all, this illusion had messed with my mind for long enough.

The analogy that was born inside the creation of "Puppet" goes so much further than my addiction. She is a dancer with life. She lives and loves and fails and succeeds at all she wants and desires. What she has failed to realize up to this point is why this whirlpool of life had so subtly consumed her when she danced so in step with the waves. We can lose ourselves inside so many things. Relationships, money, power… the list goes on. What we think controls us, unravels to reveal the truth. Only in unveiling this deception can we see that our addictions have a deeper-seated truth. We are the puppet alright, but we are also the puppeteer.

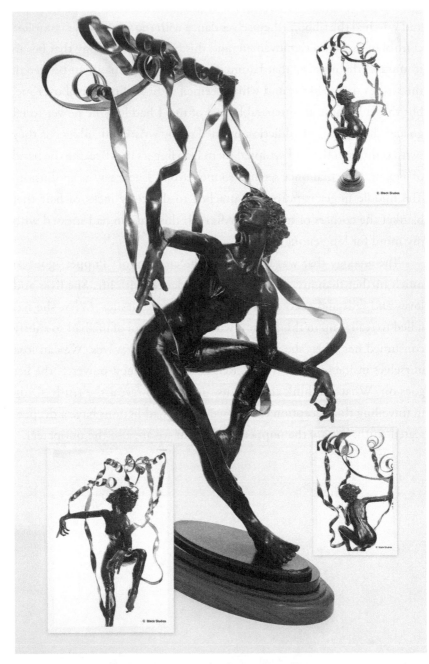

Puppet—21" x 40" x 24" limited edition bronze

Chapter 4
BUTTERFLIES AND HURRICANES

No matter what battles were going on in my life, I always yearned for and welcomed the opportunities to make a difference in someone's life or situation.

It's easy to think that we have no significance when we look at the "Big Picture" around us. From what goes on inside each code of DNA to the movement of solar systems in the universe, it all looks so overwhelmingly huge.

Focusing on the material makeup that forms a mass or the tiny bricks of fear in the giant wall of an illusion of power can tend to make us feel so insignificantly small in comparison. Seeing the glory inside the fibers of a single feather that lift a bird into flight seems to have nothing to do with the simultaneous dance of the entire flock. But there are proven points that make me think that even the flick of a finger can cause a tidal wave and that inside every fiber there is a link that gives rise to the dance happening on as large of a scale as we want to think possible. I believe that we play an instrument in this orchestra, and that every tiny thought is heard and reverberated in a cause and effect generation of movement or vibration that triggers worlds of differences. This is otherwise known as the "butterfly effect".

Just to see a flock of flamingos perform their rare and beautiful dance, or to watch the synchronized movements in a swarm of bees, a school of fish or a herd of buffalo is evidence enough that a connection lies deep within all of us, and that this tiny bit makes a huge difference on the whole. Somehow, when we get down to business and look deeper into who we really are... the perspective gets a lot closer, and having an effect on the world does not seem to be such an impossible feat after all.

Did you ever get up so close to a painting that your focus is strictly on a brush stroke and the painting as a whole becomes a blur inside that moment? This is the artist's perspective. With somewhat of a whole in mind, the artist creates beauty inside every stroke. I've fallen in love with brush strokes. They take on certain colors that flow aimlessly... creating some emotional stir within me that wants to pick through the smallest detail in them and find a painting within the painting. Somehow when the abstract coalesces and the colors take on a life of their own, my own thoughts stop and a whole new world takes over.

This is where God lives, the very fiber of who we are, inside the quantum soup that makes up the perception of reality through our senses. To see beauty in every brush stroke and every drop of rain and to realize that inside every moment there is a massive work of art created just for us is a form of satori—a sudden flash of awareness or individual enlightenment.

I love to sink into the warm realization that inside every moment there is a giant painting created just for me—right in front of my eyes. After all, I am the only one standing in the spot I am standing in at any given moment. The slightest move changes the whole painting. Just this one tiny realization could be enough to make me spend hours, but most likely seconds, admiring a single leaf in a state of bliss. But there is a world of leaves, a mass of individuals and a plethora of experiences. The trick is to realize the beauty in every brush stroke, but see the painting as a whole.

We are a part of a whole. I used to clam up when someone mentioned quantum physics. To me it sounded like too much dry toast…or too much factual information and not enough play. This was not true in the least. Anytime there is a creative aspect put into any equation, my heart lights up. Well, it just so turns out that both math and science are based on creativity. Everything is. When it all gets boiled down, the deepest parts of what we are made up of become inexplicable brush strokes taking on their own individual beauty that will not fit into a box. Everything has its own agenda, its own free will, yet it all orchestrates into a symphony of consequences that we call life.

There are different levels of what we call our reality. There is our physical existence, our outer shell which is what our senses react to on a daily basis. Then there is the cellular level, the molecular level, the atomic level (electrons and protons), and our consciousness—the observation that brings reality full circle.

The word "quantum" comes from the Latin word "quantus," which means "how much". In physics—the study of physical forces and qualities—a quantum is the minimum amount of any physical entity involved in an interaction. Broken down, quantum physics is the study of the smallest stuff and the way that it dances with the universe as whole. We are made up of tiny particles and waves of energy. Actually we are waves of energy reacting to an observation and collapsing into a specific time and space. There must be an interaction in order for us to exist. We are a choice. We are a massive bundle of possibility.

Inside the world of quantum mechanics there is something called "superpositioning". To explain superpositioning, scientists have observed that a single particle (particles are the tiny bits of matter that make up who we are) can be in many places at once. How many times have we all wished to be in many places at once? It turns out that this is exactly the world we live in. The only time a particle becomes singular or the one possibility is through observation. We are who we are because this is the conclusion that everyone has come to. We know this on a philosophical level as well. We have the ability to change the perception of others, therefore changing how we are perceived, but particles are the essential physical element that perceptively perform as our philosophies do.

There are millions of possibilities here. Actually many more than that, but this is how we tick on the smallest level. If I would have turned left at the light instead of right my whole life may have changed. That is the philosophical reasoning... but to realize this what is actually happening in a physical sense is a mind boggling realization. Think of it. Each tiny bit is a piece of a possible reality interacting with the other tiny bits in a wave of frequency that our heart song sings. Through the simple act of intention we can change the molecular structure of water. The power of what we say is even greater, and when action comes into play, superpositioning becomes the one reality that we are observing.

Another amazing fact in the quantum world, is that the tiny particles that we observe can appear and disappear in a single moment. This could be a thought of as someone disappearing and reappearing in a singular moment being thought of—which in effect, is time travel. This could also be travel through space. Our thoughts re-appear in someone else's thoughts making them think of us. In another relationship explained in the quantum world, two particles that have a relationship can be separated and no matter how far away they are, they react to the same stimuli. This is called "entanglement". A scientist named Rupert Sheldrake began a series of experiments on entanglement on a larger scale. In observing dogs, he wondered why they are always in the same spot when we come home. After countless hours of research and experimentation, he came to the conclusion that the moment the owner thinks of coming home, the dog has a reaction and moves to the spot, or shows signs of knowing this. This happens instantaneously despite the distance or space between them.

What if we treated emotions as our sixth sense? Is it just as easy as that? Are emotions the connections that bind us, the mortar in the illusionary brick wall that morphs and bends like a giant grid spread throughout the fabric of space and time? If so, can we rely on them, control them and even alter the larger picture of reality with them?

Emotions are extremely hard to control, impossible it seems, on the larger scale in the melting pot of personalities in which we exist. Individually, I believe we are able to work with them constructively and that becoming a better individual has a huge effect on this entire universe. However, letting our emotions control us can have an adverse effect. Each and every one of us are extremely important and we do make a difference with every action we take, and every word we speak.

In a documentary on the Oprah channel, Maya Angelou, said that she treats words as things. They can seep into your furniture or your skin and hide in out carpets so she was extremely sensitive about what was said under her roof. She would not allow bad-mouthing of anyone or anything to be present in her household. Her life story is amazing. She became a mute because she thought her words killed the man who raped her, only to later become one of the world's most prolific speakers and inspire masses with her beautiful words.

I believe strongly in the power of prayer or speaking intentions into reality.

Playground Prayers and Valentine's Day Wishes

One fine day in Pittsburgh, PA, when my oldest daughter was much younger, we made plans to go to the playground. After a full day of spending it running around and doing my errands it started getting late. She had been so patient with me, never saying a word as one thing led to another thing and the short list of things I had to get done before we ran off to play got longer and longer. Then, it started to thunderstorm. The top was down on my Jeep so I pulled over and quickly put it back on. I looked at her and caught her sunken display of disappointment that had rolled in along with the dark clouds. I would have done anything to make the sun come out again. So I did what I knew I could do.

"Mikayla, lets pray for a hole in the sky!" I exclaimed excitedly without even thinking. Her whole face lit up like a shiny bright star with beautiful blonde curly rays of light matching her hair. With the innocence of a typical 5 year-old, she let out a little bellow of a laugh and we both giggled out a prayer. The rain was beating the streets, yet we continued to drive through the thunder towards the playground singing songs of sunshine.

When we rounded the corner to the street that led up to our favorite spot, things looked bleak. A flash of lightning and a big boom made my heart skip… but as we turned the corner once more, there it was! Sure enough, there was a freaking hole in the sky! A ray of sunshine just seemed to scream "Ha-ha! There ya go!" from the heavens above, and we ran to play on as many things as we could. A wall of rain surrounded us and seemed to stay just outside the perimeter of the playground long enough for the two of us to be filled with wonder. The rain eventually made its way in and forced us out, but our hearts were filled and we had witnessed our own private miracle. We laughed all the way home.

Years later, I was celebrating Valentine's Day in Key West, Florida while doing a gallery show. Although I usually maintain high hopes, Valentine's Day has traditionally been a rough holiday for me. Whether from a bad memory or the wrong attitude, it's not made my list of favorite holidays. I decided to see it differently. I changed my tune, lightened up and decided to let all the love around me sink in instead of being a bad sport about it. Fortunately, Key West provides a perfect atmosphere for this. The sunny warmth of uninhibited laid back smiles seem to permeate the air itself. I had been talking to some artist friends about the power of intention and told them the story about the miracle in the playground.

After listening to the story, we all decided to go and watch the sunset from a restaurant's pier. My friends asked me what I would like to wish for in my sky for Valentine's Day on my last night in Key West. It was actually the 13th of February and I was leaving for Seattle the next day... destined to be on a plane ride all day long on Valentine's Day. Nonetheless, I told them I would be happy to see a beautiful sunset... but that a heart-shaped cloud sure would be cool too. And with that, out went the spoken request for a heart shaped cloud in the sky for Valentine's Day.

When we got to the pier on the edge of ocean, we looked skyward but couldn't really find any cloud that even loosely resembled a heart. Usually you can make out something; a heart is a really simple shape. But nothing resembled one. It was a beautiful sunset though.

The next day I spent the morning on the beach and had to rush to catch my plane. A Valentine's Day pink taxi even picked me up to take me to the airport. I didn't realize how late I really was. I had had such a great conversation with another of my new friends that I was still lost in it when I got on the plane to Miami.

As I got off the plane and rushed to catch the connecting flight I spotted a really great-looking flight attendant waiting there at the end of the tunnel for me. The thought crossed my mind that this Valentine's Day was not as uneventful as I had anticipated. So far, it had been an amazing love filled few days. Everyone that I had met in Key West seemed to have their hearts on fire. Spending time with people who were in love had only served to enhance my romantic notions, instead of my usual bah-humbug attitude towards everyone who was in love. It was an imperceptible change, but one which nonetheless had amazing effects on my psyche.

At the entrance of the plane, I stopped in the little bubble part of the tunnel to open my suitcase and get out a sweater. After all, I was soon going to be entering the land of frost. It was February and I was still in my bikini top from the beach. The nice handsome man asked with a sly grin if I needed any help, and this just kept getting better. I smiled back and replied that I had my bases covered. He asked where my seat was, which was somewhere in the back of the plane.

"Oh, you don't want to sit way back there, do you?" he politely asked, sly grin still intact.

I sly-smiled him back... "I will sit wherever you would like me to sit." Another grin just as big revealed his sparkling white smile. He then told me he would see if there was a better spot for me.

I ended up in seat 3A. A first-class seat on a plane that had just returned from France. The seats fully recline all the way back into a sleeping position. This happened to be his station, so he brought me cookies, chocolate kisses, and some really nice French Champagne that I declined to indulge in. It was heaven. My Valentine's Day was saved! Finally, I was getting the exact thing I'd wished for every Valentine's Day. All I needed now was for him to strip down to a couple of fig leaves and feed me some grapes with a big palm leaf waving my worries away! Just as he finished passing out the hot towels, I looked out my window.

The view from above was no less than spectacular. There on the horizon, was a beautiful sunset filled with every color in full brilliance. In between me and the sun was what looked like the fluffiest blue quilt of cottony clouds I had ever laid eyes on. It was an amazing light blue color. I exhaled in such veneration that I was almost in tears. Two years previous, I had wandered too close to death and the thought of what I would have missed in this moment, and in every one of the moments since, was bringing me into silent and humble reverence.

Just then, as we glided through this sunset draped sea of beauty, I noticed what looked like a vast canyon coming up on the cottony fabric of clouds. As we slowly approached the colors of the sunset were making their grand finale of brilliance in mind-bending colors and the dip or hole in the clouds started to take shape... it was a giant heart! There, outside my window in a first-class seat that came so unexpectedly was a giant valentine.

I still get lumps in my throat when I tell that story. I think God loves appreciation as much as we do and I will be forever grateful for that special, heaven-sent Valentine. I don't think there is a man on this planet that can top that one.

I painted a picture of it from memory as soon as I got home. The flight attendant said that this formation was caused from another plane when it breaks through the clouds. In the planes wake, the wind from its body splits the clouds open. Although he had seen it before he said that it's very rare. The weather conditions have to be just right.

Caption: Watercolor sketch of my favorite valentine ever.

This story, as well as so many others, leads me to believe that our words, our thoughts and our emotions can be the catalyst in determining the destiny of each of our lives on this planet.

Silence

Words can be powerful things.

In the Bible it says that God spoke the world into existence. In Australia, a ritual called "bone pointing" can kill a man in a couple of days by chanting a curse and pointing a bone. Placebos have been documented to cure everything from cancer to heart disease and then completely reversed when the patient learns that it was just a "sugar pill".

Words spoken in haste can lead to deeper and darker avenues than what was originally felt in the emotion of the moment. There are many times that I have had to go back and fix something that was said because I did so without thinking. Pulling the foot out of my mouth seems so much more painful than if I could have just sewn my mouth shut in the first place.

On the other hand, the beauty lost in the words I could have said equally serves to pick at my soul. In my early 20's I painted "Silence". I was in a relationship with someone who never seemed to want to listen to what I had to say. It hurt when he would tell me to shut up so that he could study. I was longing to be understood, and was lost in my own walls of silence. In this painting are fears, losses and silent moments when something should have been said, yet silence prevailed.

In looking back, I have wished that I have been a reminder over the years to the ones I loved, of someone who saw them as they truly were, and the beauty and potential that was only a breath away. We never know when those words could save someone from a fate not worth taking. It is a reminder to me to stand up for what I know to be right and good, while having the courage to speak up against the wrongs I see in the world.

There is a really beautiful prayer that I like to say in times of question: "God, grant me the serenity to accept the things I cannot change, the courage to change the things I can, and the wisdom to know the difference…"

Caption: **"Silence"**—*36"x 60" oil painting*

A Lesson from India

Nowadays, I learn so much from going to church. I'd always enjoyed the energy I experienced there as a kid and again, now that I'm older. My journey wasn't a continuous line of faith though. I strayed off the path and stopped going to church all together after our pastor had made a big deal out of his daughter getting pregnant out of wedlock. All of a sudden, church looked ugly to me.

It took almost a decade before I would step foot in a church again. I had not faced the sheer humiliation that my pastor's daughter had felt, but I loathed rejection and judgment not only of myself, but of others as well. What I failed to see was my own ego. Leaders, pastors, teachers… they are all human and they make mistakes too. Just because we put someone on a pedestal does not make them infallible. I let one mistake be a judgment call for every religion out there, especially Christianity. Judgment alone causes more pain and separation than some perceived infractions. A little love, respect and empathy would serve so much better in these instances.

In the same respect, I hope that anything I say about God or prayer does not deter you from reading this book. If the word God bothers you, forgive me. That is simply the name I grew up with and I have seen way too much evidence to deny the existence of an all-encompassing creative intelligence. This is not a book on religion, nor do I think I have all the answers to any questions that demand absolution. In the realm of spirituality, I simply do not know anything that I can call a solid fact, but that is where faith takes its place to allow me to open my mind to all possibilities and has answered my curiosity in better ways than listening to any one individual who demands that they alone are right. My hope is that you take the information you hear in the same way. Openly, but with discernment.

One day in church we had a guest speaker. A man named Dr. Ivan Satyavrata, who leads a mission of mercy in Calcutta, India. He said that in this capital city, the poverty ratio is overwhelming. Eighty percent of the people survive there on just 2 dollars a day, and another small percentage on only 1 dollar a day. Nearly 20,000 children a day receive meals and basic care through the auspices of his mission.

When asked if there is ever a feeling of hopelessness, the good doctor replied, "Yes, but I have learned to pray this one simple prayer.... God, you have a problem. If you need my help or need to use me in any way, I am here."

Dr. Satyavrata said that the hunger and poverty is just a symptom of a much larger disease. The people hunger for spirituality—they suffer from a lack of love.

This, to me, is so profound. I want to cure the world of hunger and solve our poverty problems just as much as the next heart filled with compassion. There are many of us, more than we know. But sending food in a box, or money in an envelope only puts a bandage on a gushing artery. All this helps, don't get me wrong. The problem has grown so big that continuous funds are needed just to keep people alive, but in order to begin healing; there is a realization that must occur.

In twelve-step programs, they call this Step One. We admitted we were "powerless to the addiction {to this pain, suffering and poverty} and that life has become unmanageable." People in Calcutta cannot be blamed for some sort of addiction to poverty; this is not what I mean. I'm simply looking at this through the eyes of an artist, creating a new way to see it.

I suffered from alcoholism, and while I think there is much more justification in blaming myself for drinking than in blaming a starving child for their own hunger, there is a common denominator here that I feel is incredibly important. Just as I could not cure my drinking alone, a starving child in India cannot cure his pain with money and food from an online donation.

Love saved me. Hands-on, face-to-face tears of compassion. I believe we suffer from lack of a love that can only be fixed in a hands-on manner. No cyber-hugs, Internet love gushing or cold video kisses. This link in digital communication is amazing and fantastic and has brought to light many of the world's problems as well as solutions, but it has also cuts us off from reality. It's completely normal to see a person fused to their phone in the middle of an intimate dinner with family and friends nowadays. But for the sake of creating change and making the world an amazing place—reach out and look at the person next to you! Hold their hand and smile into their eyes. Just looking into a store clerks eyes and smiling when you wish them a nice day has an overwhelming effect. Most of us never even look up from our wallets or purses to say hello.

I think that with repeated news of gun-slinging loners waltzing into public domains to take the lives of innocent bystanders, the recognition of a Step One reality in society today has begun.

We are one on a journey towards a greater existence. One soul that strays affects us all; one soul that sees the light and follows it with passion does the same. Creativity is the source of love. Step Two in the twelve-step programs dealing with addiction taught me about blind faith, the portal to creativity. "We came to believe that a power greater than ourselves could restore us to sanity..." Addiction is insanity. Believing that every morning you have to wake up to the same boring routine, or follow a path in lock-step to your addiction is insanity.

Choice is only one thought away. Simply clearing the path, believing that the day will just be different enough to change your destiny opens you to the portal. A simple step one /step two prayer in the face of frustration can send life twirling into a path of wonder and delight... "God I have no power over this... or like Dr. Satyavrata—God, there is a problem..."

This—*this* is freedom, letting go, opening a space. Without space there is no room for the new solution to come and work its magic. God must see an opening. This is the power of the gift of free will. We came, we suffered, we struggled, cried and stomped our feet. Then we sank, hopelessly to the bottom of the tank, giving in to the inevitable thought of the flushing of the toilet....poor little fish. But wait... in a last ditch attempt to gasp for oxygen... out of the depths of despair... here in this nowhere land of death and destruction is where the miracle of life sits and waits for the small utterance of one tiny shimmer of faith. "I believe" is all that it needs to hear. Amazing miracles and stories of heroism... acts of true courage and astounding life accomplishments have come from the very bottoms of fishbowls everywhere. You don't have to see it to believe it; you have to believe it to *see*.

Chapter 5
LOVE AND FEAR

The Opposites

Addiction and creativity are as polar opposite as heaven and hell. I often used to wonder if there was some relation between the two. So many creative people seem to have had an issue with it.

An addiction happens when a person loses control and becomes dependent upon a substance or emotion to be who they are. They are no longer themselves and are controlled by a fear that is only masked by the facade of the cloak they cover the pain with. It is the opening for every kind of possession of soul and/or spirit.

People can be addicted to pain and suffering just as easy as they can be to drugs and alcohol. Just because it is not ingested orally or otherwise does not make emotional addiction obsolete. These kinds of addictions can be just as dangerous as the obvious ones. There is a common denominator that connects them all. The core of all addictions is the fear. Fear of being oneself and being judged for it, fear of being persecuted, rejected, unloved and untouched. Fear runs rampant in today's society, unfortunately, because we lack connection and have been coerced into a consumer mentality. If we feel judged by appearance we can have that surgically removed or enhanced. If we feel lonely we can go shopping to buy things that will make us more attractive. We (myself included) can be buried alive by dependencies on self-pity, narcissism, greed, gluttony… the list goes on. All the while unaware that the shovel is in our own hands.

Creativity, on the other hand is driven by love. Perhaps the reason that so many artists are drawn to the effects of alcohol and drugs lies with their compulsive attraction to a loss of control and inhibition. When I am inside the flurry of a creative storm, a passion drives me. Love fills me and what evolves remains to be seen, waiting for its final brush-stroke or soft sculptural touch. It is as much a mystery to me as it is to anyone, how a blank canvas or lump of clay become something so much more. I only know that if I remain an open book the pages will get filled and the canvas will be covered in color. But I had to first do the footwork and learn the basics of art, knowing all the while that at some point I would have enough of a foundation to let that knowledge breathe, become instinctual and finally let go of the reins and allow that passion to take over my fingertips like a herd of wild horses.

These polar opposite reactions are the forbidden fruit inside the Garden of Eden. In the universe of our minds there is a choice. Once bitten, the gift of free-will sets us off on a journey down the road of knowledge. We now see the darkness as well as the light. And the darkness has tricked us into thinking we are no longer a part of this light; that we are somehow cut off.

Broken down, fear is just a sensory perception that is delivered to the neurons in the brain through either thought or sight, touch, smell, taste or sound. If fear is induced through one of the five senses, appropriate action is usually taken involuntarily through the nervous system. Luckily we have an autopilot system set up in our brain designed to run things when we do not have the time to rationally think things through. This is called the cerebellum. The cerebellum produces the proper neurotransmitters or polypeptides which are chemicals produced to induce reaction. For example, adrenaline is pumped into our bodies when we need to run from an attacking bear. This is a prime example of a case where fear is a good thing.

The fear that drives addictions and disconnects us from society is a false fear. This is the fear that can start sentences in your mind with things like, "Here we go again, you are just going to…blah, blah, blah" or "oh no…they will think I am…na-na, na-na" or "she always does… poo, poo, poo". It scares us away from trying new things, wastes way too many hours of our lives discussing things that have never happened and basing them on past issues that are just that—PAST issues. Fear based on judgment is illusion. It is either something that happened that I can do nothing about in the present or something that hasn't even happened yet. Dwelling inside of fear in any situation is living in hell.

I lived in false fear for much of my life. I worried about what everyone thought about me, I listened to fear-based criticisms about things that just don't matter unless you have an addiction to emotional trauma.

I was not only addicted to alcohol. My cell receptors were programmed to thirst for attention, emotional pain, and self-pity. What a combination…I could wallow in it with a good bottle of scotch and stay there for days, weeks and eventually was a victim of it for years. We learn to go into these dark places to escape. But when we come out, the light is brighter than it was before.

I used to beat myself up for the choices I made to escape. I felt guilty, ashamed, and wrong and believed that I was somehow sentenced to take the "easy" way out regardless. None of it however, is or was easy. Whether I dealt with life head on or drank till I could, the road less traveled is the one filled with the most wild flowers. To find the treat in the trick, I had to peel away the layers of self-centered guilt and shame. I had to give myself time to heal and find a way to share what I had learned in order to help others see the crazy beauty that sprouts nonstop from the **** fertilizer of the slayed dragons. Only in this would I be able to see the beauty myself, instead of wallowing in self-pity.

However, choosing love is not as easy as it sounds. Fear is the easy way out. To choose love is to dig deep within and find the truth. It is the only right answer when every question is painstakingly asked. When I ask myself what the true intention is in any decision, the best and hardest answer is based on love. If I know that I'm in a relationship that is only hurting the other person, but I don't want to leave because I'll be alone, I know now that this is a freight train headed straight for a train wreck of unhappiness. It's way harder to leave someone BECAUSE you love them. It is equally hard to let your children make decisions that you know may not be the best for them. I'm a fan of the "boy in the bubble" concept and wish I could build one around my girls. But this will not help them. Love is tough, I would have never dreamed that the biggest rewards that love has to offer comes from letting go.

In certain circumstances, I've completely confused the word love with lust. I had a hard time distinguishing where the line was or if there even needed to be one for that matter. I've always been a passionate person. Some people have no trouble holding back their passions and I am a duly sworn member of that club. Whether it was because some are afraid of getting hurt or for the sake of letting someone else go before them in a holy sacrifice, holding back on the reins of that wild stallion will still give you a ride – it just won't give you the exhilaration of having both feet in the stirrups.

Albrecht Durer's drawing of the praying hands has such a beautiful story behind it. His brother sacrificed his own passion to send Albrecht to art school and worked for four years in the mines to help him pay for school. It was a decision made on the toss of a coin. Both brothers were artists in a family of 18 children, but one had to work to help pay for the others' passion. When Albrecht returned from art school and proposed a toast to his brother, excited to now send him to the same school with the proceeds from his successful commissions, tears streamed from his brothers eyes. It was too late. The years in the mine had crushed his hands and they were twisted with arthritis.

I grew up with a picture of those praying hands in my house and never knew how amazing they truly were. They are a symbol of love.

I live for passion. It's what I do for a living. When it grabs me in the middle of the night I jump into awareness and eagerly greet it at the door. Sometimes I roll over too tired to get up and paint, but if it is strong enough, nothing can hold back the urge. In some instances when the floodgates of creativity are opened, it is like love courses through my bloodstream, producing a pulse that cannot wait to find its heartbeat on canvas. When the intention of letting go, breathing life and exhaling hope is rushing through those gates this is creativity at its finest. This is love in motion. Creativity becomes a beautiful river of unpolluted, untainted, unrestricted freedom. Whether it comes through on canvas, in clay, or through the sonnet of words or notes on a score—its source is the same.

Rivers of Love

A sculpture I named "The Moldau" was made while listening to the orchestral poem of the same name by Bedrich Smetana, and illustrated that gush of emotion perfectly. In a music appreciation class that I snuck into, I learned the story behind the music. Its melody tells the story of a river that runs through the Czech Republic from the river's perspective. In the "story" you can hear the meshing of two streams into one, one cold and the other from a hot spring. It rushes past wedding celebrations and castles, battles and their aftermath of destruction. It plummets over falls and trickles into streams, over rocks and every sound is recorded inside this lyrical symphony.

One day Smetana's piece found itself streaming through the speakers of my stereo and plummeting its way into a large mass of clay. When I listened to the instruments tell their story of the two rivers becoming one, I felt a passionate anxiousness, a profound feeling of not being able to get close enough. When skin and flesh are in the way, an overpowering urge to meld the two into one another became a dance of one as my fingers shaped what became the music in shape and form. So I sculpted that emotion, and captured the passion in mud. Both love and lust can contain elements of passion. Distinguishing passion's origin and a gutsy truthful investigation of intention will reveal which of the two is in the driver's seat.

Caption: "The Moldeau"

Lust will lie and make us think that it is a passionate river, but don't let it fool you. It is a backed-up sewage pipe. It comes from the selfish, needy side that only wishes to rob and steal away true passion. All logic, sense, and responsibility slip through the stinky cracks. The spark that sets lust on fire burns deep down and gets itself entangled in the heart as it passes by. Its fire burns hard and fast and destroys every living, breathing thing in its path. It lives to take and will stop at nothing to do so.

It can continue to fester inside for years and can lead to addiction, depression, anger, self-pity and self-destruction while manifesting itself in everything from pornography to chocolate indulgences. It feasts, never once stopping to replenish what it takes in its full-forced drive to destroy everything and anything in its way. Not until it is often too late, do we see the path of destruction this raging ball of burning sewage has left behind. It feels like a gushing burst of wonderment in the beginning, but two or three months later, sometimes sooner than that... it's a blur of messy information and always holds a painful and sorrowful exit waiting.

It's not easy to distinguish a difference if there is no protective wall of time and patience around the fires of passion. It took me a long time to learn this. Many heartbreaks and broken dreams later, it turns out that the advice to take it slow is very GOOD advice.

Love is a simple and beautiful thing that is meant to be left to happen of its own accord. I've never had to "work" to creating anything. I had to work HARD to learn anatomy, how to draw, the mechanics of color theory, motion and what things go where, but never at creating. I think that love works in a similar way. We have to work at being better human beings towards one another on many facets, but love falls across those facets like water over a glistening, gentle fall when the rocks have worn down enough to let it flow through.

This poses quite a struggle for me—letting things flow. I'm the kind that would rather eat the chocolate laxative and make stuff happen. Turns out nature provides a much more beneficial result with a proper diet and exercise. This wonderful analogy spreads to every aspect in life.

The Evolution of Love

In 2007, I began working on a series of four fountains called the "Evolution of Love". It has not been completed to this day, but the journey is worth some explanation. In the series, I wanted to represent mankind's spiritual evolution, the evolution of the soul, the encompassing universe and the very nature of miracles.

I designed the series to be seen in a succession, but nevertheless one that evolves, so that no matter where the viewer starts, each sculpture has a life of its own.

In looking up different philosophies and stories of love I found similarities and merged them together in the first sculpture of the series. Much like the "Moldau", my fingers fused a couple together as one, simply because I love that feeling. It's one of the most passionate expressions of love. I found a lot of people who felt the same way throughout time. These included writings of mankind being one with God, or spirit. In Aristophanes' speech from Plato's symposium, called "The Origin of Love" couples were once fused together forming one creature, and all powerful…so much so, that they tried to overthrow the gods. In doing so, they were separated into two and have forever been searching for their missing half. There are so many beautiful writings on this. In the Bible, God takes a rib from Adam to form Eve. I wanted to encompass the overall feeling of being one and complete in the beginning piece.

In the second piece, an explosion happens, a drastic change, the knowledge of the dark side… and we are sent off in a spirit of love and with a gift of free-will. The pain of the separation was meant for us to learn a greater appreciation of love, and of the unity that is still within us. There is a power within each of us that will guide us to our destiny if we listen. For some it takes a traumatic event, for some knowledge brought through years of pain... there are a lot of ways to wake up to that epiphany. It is the moment when all ego is lost, and an amazing blanket of love swaddles the soul. The moment each of us enters the matrix, realizing that nothing is impossible in the light of God or the Creator, this is the light found in uncovering truth. This second fountain represents the moment of the fall...or the surrender.

In the separation... the third sculpture, there is a wall of water separating the couple. Isolation becomes a self-imposed illusion. We chose it; separating ourselves from each other because of religion, wars, prejudices, hatred, jealousy, all forms of the ego the by-product of fear. The deception is as solid as we want to make it... but inside the truth we can see the transparency of it all. In fact, we all remain connected and have never been separated. We can reach through the wall. The wall is the connection, the spiritual soup, the quantum, the matrix or in the Sanskrit, the "Akasha"— meaning both its elemental and metaphysical senses.

I wanted the fourth fountain to represent the transformation of body and soul into spirit, and the awakening to our own capacity to care, to create, and to transform this planet and all that live here into a world beyond imagination. I wanted to envision what could be and put it to form. However, it's hard to sculpt heaven. I realize I could never give its vastness and glory the justice it deserves on this plane of existence. Although I want to delve into this one a bit more, so far this last sculpture has two angels embracing and spiraling up through the fountain. Their wings fuse together, once again expressing this desire to be one with all. Water would then jet up from a base with life on earth reaching up, striving for the union of peace.

Interestingly enough, I started this sculpture because a friend suggested I do a piece on love. The suggestion at that time spilled through my mind like rotten milk coagulating through my system and threatening to exit looking a bit like vomit. I was not in love. I was wallowing in self-pity. I'd been in and out of more than my share of dead-end relationships, chewed up and spit out, used, rejected and flattened like a... not even a pancake... more like, a crepe run over by a Mack truck. Just the thought of happy couples brought on a taste of hurl that I remembered so well from my drinking days. So I decided to do it.

This a sketch I made of the four fountains. I don't envision them all together. More in a garden setting with pathways to each. The rest of the sculptures remain unfinished to this day.

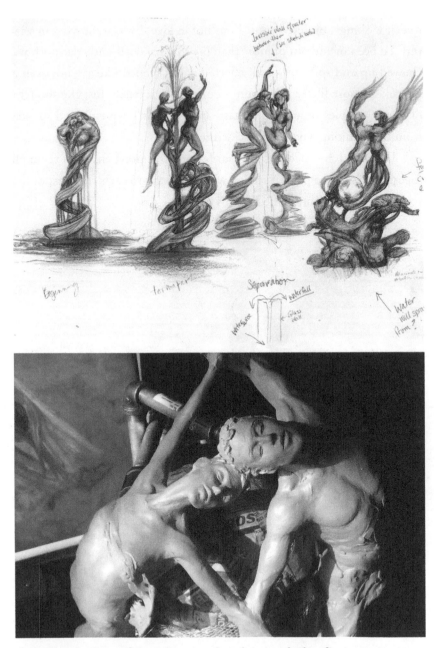

"The Evolution of Love"—my sketches and the first maquette— which is a small rough sculpture of the idea.

Soul Mates and the Abyss

If we are truly on a quest—a search for the highest form of love—then decisions have to be made that are not solely self-serving as individuals. It's easy to be selfish and impatient when others are involved. True love has none of this however. It's easy to receive, not hard.

I fall in love all the time. I can be driving down the road and catch a glimpse of Mt. Rainier in the morning light with clouds whispering to its peak and suddenly my heart fills to its brim and some of it spills out of the corners of my eyes. This happens when I let go and ride inside the wave, not trying to obstruct anything....but there is a level of love that personally, I have only found twice in my life.

There were two separate moments in time of overwhelming bliss, when two bodies are one and seem to mesh into a spectrum of light. Sex is a marvelous thing, but making love tops all corners of what I yearn for. How is it that something so beautiful can be so rare when I can be so filled with love so easily?

Herein lies the question of the soul mate. Is this a myth? I used to think so. I wanted to believe in something so special, in a connection so deep that it broke every boundary and that even whispering a person's name would travel through time and space and kiss their face like they were standing next to me. This connection exists. I know it does. It is far more beautiful, vast, deep and mysteriously unpredictable than even I want know and it changes form every single stinking time I try to catch it and put it in a box.

Perhaps that is all I need to know. Imagining that my thoughts alone could have an effect on someone halfway around the world used to seem almost mythical to me ten years ago. Until I could understand the physics of such things, having faith in them seemed to be beyond my grasp. I searched with a passion and answers were thrown into my lap, exactly when I had enough understanding to take it one more step, right up until now. And the beat continues. This quest of understanding has gone on for centuries, and takes on a different explanation with each new term. From the Akashic record to morphic resonance, they all seem to have some relative existence and contain amazing similarities.

In Hinduism, Akasha means the basis and essence of all things in the material world. In Sanskrit the word means "space," the very first element in creation. One of my favorite definitions on the subject was from Madame Blavatsky, who defined 'Akasha' as the basis of all Universal Life "Force" Energy, created through the magical unification of the four primary elements of earth, air, fire and water to form the soul and spirit of all living beings. The Akasha contains not only a record of everything that has ever happened, but also everything that will ever come to pass in the future.

The hypothesis of "morphic resonance," according to Rupert Sheldrake suggests that natural systems, such as termite colonies, or pigeons, or orchid plants, or insulin molecules, inherit a collective memory from all previous things of their kind and is responsible for mysterious telepathy-type interconnections between organisms.

Each has its own conceptual definition and is much deeper and further explained with as much research as you want to do. I find the similarities fascinating.

I simply cannot help myself when it comes to delving into the possibilities in life. It's part of the "Akasha" within me. Much of what we really want in life can only be obtained through faith, simply by believing in a concept. If we just have the faith that our best friend benefits from our prayers...it happens. It may not be in the way we WANT it to happen, but with a pure heart filled with good intention, what is absolutely best will prevail. It's been written for centuries and it is now being explained in scientific terms on the quantum level as well.

Just thinking of someone can cause them to think of you and perhaps even call you. This is a personal favorite thing I love to do. It's like having a personal secretary that reads my mind. Having faith that this connection is a reality and not some sort of hocus pocus myth will catapult us into a higher existence where our connection will become intrinsic. We won't have to wonder anymore, we can just know. Soulmates love mutually so deep that the souls involved were designed to nurture each other's existence. It's a bond that can never be broken, and is the alpha and the omega in this wondrous journey called life.

We can find ourselves searching forever for a love that serves our purpose, for someone that fits a mold that we have morphed over a long period of time. The probabilities of such a search bringing about a one hundred percent positive result have to be next to none. Thank God no one can fit the mold. Human clay seems to have its own ideas and its own sweet life, with each of us weaving ourselves into a beautiful fabric of fate, so intricate that each little fiber changes the whole picture.

We are the artists of our own worlds, but everyone has a paintbrush and the canvas is left to unfold and transform into a melody and eventually a symphony of reactions to stimulate the senses. This beautiful ability to transform is like that of an abstract work of art. The colors left to blend with themselves or a stroke of the brush left to just be, now seems so much more beautiful to me than what I saw in my mind's eye as my finished masterpiece. Overworked art has its place and molded individuals do too. But I am now leaning towards the abstract lifestyle and ready to let go of the reins to let the wild horses run free. I want to go where I have not been and to see what I have not seen. The only way to do this is to let go.

Actively searching for that special someone seems to be exactly like purposeful painting or sculpting an exact portrait. The end result can be beautiful, but it has no life of its own. It asks no questions to drive it forward. It is simply is what it is—a painting of something or a portrait of someone. It can have character, and it can take on the lives of the viewers as they place themselves behind some question that they see arise such as the Mona Lisa's smile.

All artwork will forever have this going for it. Even the painting hanging on your brother's wall by Aunt Matilda of the faraway barn in the open field painted with horrible color, the lamest composition and a really poor excuse of drafting skills may hide behind its doors, her emotional longing to be far away from the life she chose. Inside the field under the grassy nature she found her heart wandering away from her overbearing and boring husband. Perhaps she could feel the wind wisping through her young and beautiful locks of golden hair and could forget the coarse grays now in their place. Inside the barn was a world of hidden treasure... her first kiss, a long lost love, and a horse that used to carry her to fairytale adventures filling her heart with magic and sweetness that no one had ever really seen. A taste of this freedom may have fallen into the embers of your brother's heart and with the untimely death of Aunt Matilda, her longing lives on, burning a new flame.

Art has beautiful sonnets and heartfelt dreams written between the lines. It doesn't take anything but an opening in the heart of the viewer to be able to read the passions and stories behind the paint. Each brushstroke carries its own interpretation of the storyline. There is no right way or wrong way. It is where you as the viewer find your most beautiful secrets.

Chapter 6

KISSED THE WRONG FROG

I have never been married. I've been in and out of relationships and have held the dream of the happily ever after, only to watch it sift through my fingers and blow away with the rest of the sand on the beach. I'm sure that everyone starts off a marriage with the thought of forever as a soft comfortable place to rest their long weary lives upon. Then one day they roll over only to find that there is an uncomfortable, unlikeable pea in the mattress.

How horrible would it be to marry the "wrong one"? To one day wake up and as your eyes slowly erase the blur of dreams so quickly forgotten, they are snapped into reality. Memories of a similar sleeping beauty at your side seem so distant and as you roll over to look at the familiar form, a thought enters your mind, "What are you doing in my bed?" They started out to be the Snow White princess or the proverbial knight in shining armor...so what is this beast doing here? I've had circumstances like this, but an easy solution always followed, tinged by months of aching guilt and heartache that are never worth the night of debauchery.

Perhaps one hot, blistering summer afternoon after a typical systematic, never-changing routine of a day you see what could be "the real one". He rolls up, free as the wind itself, while your arms are packed with groceries and you're screaming at Sleeping Beauty Jr. to stop torturing the other Sleeping Beauty Jr. His teeth sparkle and gleam in the hot afternoon sun as he turns and smiles at you.

It all starts so simple. Maybe he asks to help you with your groceries. Or offers a bit of advice that turns out to be the greatest bit of parental wisdom that you've ever heard. When a brand new pretty package enters the view stream it can be hard to stop your mouth from hanging at the hinges. You watch him drift back through the afternoon light....cutting it in two.

Mmmm....The irony of it all. The Wonderful World of Daydreams has been well-travelled by my imagination. Later the thoughts come rolling in like a welcome home hug from your mother. Over the next few hours...days, then weeks, you find your mind drifting back to that stranger. His halo grows bigger, your time with him longer, and a new world starts to form itself around him. Especially when your significant other does one of those things that instantly annoys you. Your time alone becomes indispensable. It's the only time you have to daydream about Mr. or Miss Wonderful.

I can only guess that many, if not all people have experienced this innocent "affair of the mind". Lord knows I have. The trouble with being an artist is that you can even make one up. This is never anything like a real human being. I have run into total strangers and instantly been drawn to them by some "unknown" connection. I have some friends for life that have happened by galleries and met me in a conversation over art. They've become like family. But this is totally separate. An affair of the mind is much more like my artist's imaginings.

The world inside the imagination is an easy place to visit, especially when the world around you seems bleak and lacks what you desire to be there. After the glamor of the new relationship wears away and the familiarity becomes all too comfortable, the bread can go stale. Left to the elements of human nature, it's often inevitable that the once nail biting anticipation just to see each other seeps into an irreversible downward spiral. By the time the bread realizes it's been taking on a staleness, it's all too often too late. Besides, what is a stale hunk of bread supposed to do about being compared to a hot crossed bun, fresh, and sweet, right out of the oven?

Self-pity takes its rightful stand defending your every perceived right to sneak away. Poor little frog. Should have married the right princess—one that would appreciate all your efforts, your hard work... like the little tadpole at the office. She sees all the beauty that your queen on the throne just seems to overlook. When her royal highness is out spending the fruits of all your hard earned efforts on the stupid things that just don't matter, or perhaps boringly scrimping them off to savings for some monotonous future, this sweet little amphibian is fully capable of changing into anything you want her to be.

It's all too easy to hear the slightest compliment like a siren in the storm when there is no sound but the wind to comfort your lonely soul. You didn't get married to be lonely and you certainly never wanted to be stuck in the same boring routine day after day. How long ago did that all begin? What were you thinking when you kissed that frog and what do you do now? Hearts ache over strangers, co-workers, or anyone else that takes on the bait at the end of your line. Most times you didn't even know you were fishing till you find yourself reeling one in.

Affairs can start in the mind, spread dark wings to reach out and encompass the body, and seep into our soul. It is easy to convince ourselves of the innocence in this age of instant access to anything twenty-four hours a day online. But what happens when the next frog and princess find that they are again polar opposites. Is it time to jump to the next lily pad once again? And the next...and the next? Pretty soon the pond can become one big melting pot of emotional blunders, failed relationships and a cesspool of stinking rotten ruined lives and broken families.

What happened to the childhood days of dreaming about Prince Charming and the happily ever after's? Are fairy tales just wishes we tell our children to calm their beating hearts after a day of news about war, starvation, and broken dreams? Is this what we live for? Is this the American Dream? Are we puppeteering our children to live a secret life in a dream world only as a means of escaping the real-life plunders and pillages of everyday society? Let them think growing up is an admirable goal. Maybe they can fix it along the way or when they get there.

No one frog can change a sewer back into a pond. True. One frog can't even expect to change the mind of his princess once she's caught sight of another. Control is not the answer. It only causes chaos, tyranny, and eventually, rebellion. Fear only feeds the fire. When it sets in, a sense of loss takes over the soul. Many of us are simply too busy worrying about something that hasn't happened and usually basing it on false pretenses. The only possible way out of the whole mess is what seeded the whole fairytale to being with.

Remember that fairytale... that fertile childhood dream? It wasn't a fairytale, those days when you skipped through the fall leaves on the way home from school, and the wind carried them off to the raging river that in real life may have been just a drainage ditch. Still, it was a magical ditch where the leaves turned to a fleet of ships and sailed off to a faraway place to conquer a new land, and start a new life... away from the land of the lost, away from this ordinary ditch.

It's not a daydream anymore. Those dried up leaves, the ocean-liners of your soul, they still long to sail the waters of your dreams. Whether it starts with taking an extra 15 minutes on your lunch break to call your spouse and tell them what makes your heart beat a little faster, or taking your parents on that long promised trip to the African Plains....start it. Don't let the news of the day water down the fresh aroma of the sweet dreams in your life just waiting to be awakened. The sun can shine all day, every day, in the corners of our minds. This is where your world begins.

Love lives and breathes....it exists all around us. We must start treating it as a paradoxical object ... so stop poking it with a stick. It's welcomingly pliable and will respond to a warm soft touch of understanding—not a branding iron of fear that insists on dancing around its perimeter.

This arms-open approach must start from within. Simply changing our own thought patterns away from fear of loneliness, self-pity and doubt to fresh perceptions of self-worth, of gratitude for what good was there all along and a fresh excitement that comes with rediscovering ourselves puts new wind in our sails. Kissing the wrong frog is often symptomatic of a lack of appreciation for what value is placed on your own self-worth. Love's perceived value is almost always something you can change from within. If the value isn't there however, walk away -to yourself, not to the next lily pad.

People are notorious for making a mess of things. And not every relationship can be fixed. Sometimes walking away is the best you can do for both parties and all the secondary parties will come to see this when it is handled in a manner of love and compassion. Consideration for children involved in divorces or any type of broken relationship should act as a guide of behavior for both of you. Even for the couples who have no children. There always seems to be a child involved, maybe it's the one within the both of you who can serve to soften the severity of the sword's edge.

A Love for Frogs

I happen to love frogs. When I was little, there was a "frog season" at the pond near our house. Baby frogs would venture out for the first time without their tadpole tails, and frogs were everywhere. Tiny, cute little things that I wanted to keep as pets. No one wants to be kept as a pet.

Our independence and individuality is usually what attracts someone in the first place.

I have an ex that hates frogs with a passion. When I heard this, my heart reached out to them even more. Perhaps it was an effort on my part to make up for his distaste in the fairytale creature that always had provided me hope. A friend spotted a small collection of frog memorabilia in my house one time and shared an acronym with me... Forever Rely On God. This reminds me to let go of the belief that my green slimy friends will ever change form enough to sit on a princely pedestal. When expectations are set free, an empty space is left for the creation of a new fairytale.

What your beliefs are on any matter are completely up to you. I find a seed of wisdom in all beliefs. Truth is what you make it. Facts often depend on who's telling the story.

Even the color of my eyes is arguable. Some people see them as blue, some people see them as brown, some people see them as yellow, and most people think they are green. In the drinking days, the predominant color was red. I have finally given up and call them rainbow. There is no point in arguing the unknown. The ego is the one who wants to be right about this. If ego is set aside, the truth of the matter can unfold as it is perceived on its own accord.

Be good to each other, respect each other's beliefs, and have an open enough mind to listen and discern what is right for you. If you act in a manner of humble understanding instead of self-righteous omniscience, people are much more willing to hear what you have to say. Remember to offer this courtesy back to them as well. One of the biggest and most amazing gifts you can give a loved one is to be still and listen. We were given two ears and one mouth for a reason.

Frogs have become little reminders to myself to appreciate wherever I am and whoever happens to be gifting me with their presence. I don't have the experience to save a marriage and have yet to experience the happily ever after. All that I know for certain is that the happiness that can be found in my own heart is easily shared. After years of pond skipping, I truly believe that I have found home... back at the beginning, the "once upon a time," where I am once again in charge of my life and am able to choose my own direction, my own storyline . This is where the fairytale writes itself new every day.

Brand New Day

"Brand new" starts to happen whenever we feel the onset of change. Change can be scary, but set the unwarranted fear aside and let the excitement of the unknown kick it up a notch. If fear is flushed out, there is empty space—free and clear to take on the newness and exciting onset of adventure into the unknown.

I love waking up with this bounce in my step. This was the inspiration behind a painting called, "Brand New Day". A photo of me was taken in front of a window in Jamaica with the morning sun pouring through the glass like a shower of rainbows, so I used it for the technical parts of the painting. It changed a lot in translation as they always do.

In painting my recollection, I remembered the warmth of those days you couldn't wait for from one day to the next. When you passionately appreciate being alive and just can't wait to greet your day to start anew.

A new start is weightless and free, so I painted her levitating. I wanted to capture what the world of imagination looks like to me sometimes when I open that door, so the leaves from the curtains become reality and spread beneath her feet, helping to hold her in this space of freedom, forgiveness, and acceptance. I painted the hands with red flowers in the middle of them to represent a beautiful reminder of the story of Jesus and his life spent to bring us all back to this place, this space, this fresh start on life given to us as we greet the morning's sun. There's a small crack in the window as a reminder of the fragility of the moment. The irony of this is that even when reality cracks through the windows of our dreams, the once closed-off portal becomes a door….ha! In the far off distance outside the window, there is a little boy picking a flower. In reality, he was throwing rocks at a cow. Artistic license.

"Brand New Day"—24"x30" oil painting

Aura of a Brand New Day

I later painted another rendition of this painting called, "Aura of a Brand New Day". Painted with the same quality of inspiration, in this one, there is a hidden element. This painting was the birth of my discovery of phosphorescence suspended in oil color. There has always been a question of permanence in using phosphorescence. We have yet to find out if suspending them in the oil mediums will last for centuries, but in doing some research, I discovered that they break down when exposed to air or water. By using an oil suspension, neither of these will affect it and they may even last longer than the lightfast pigments that have been used to make color for paints for centuries.

By the time of this new rendition, I'd traveled much more, seen much more and was even entering into the sunset half of my life. I lived in a very rainy section of the country blessed by the beauty that lots of rain brings, but I missed blue skies and the matching water of the tropical places I had been to. In this one, I can see the ocean. And in this one I could watch the moon rise over the horizon greeting me with all the wisdom that trekking through the darkness can bring. In the bright light of day we are blind to richness and fullness in the full moons of reflection that can only come to us when the clouds are cleared and we choose to find the light inside the experience of darkness.

"Aura of a Brand New Day"—30"x40" oil painting as well as what it looks like in the dark.

Chapter 7
ESCAPE ARTIST

Escaping from reality is not necessarily a bad thing. I do it all the time inside my art-whether it is in a brush stroke, through a lump of clay or poured out through a keyboard—I am lost inside of that world. So much so, that what goes on around me often goes completely unnoticed. I have to make a conscious effort to remember not to start anything on the stove or to leave water running and have learned not to operate heavy machinery (except for the occasional chainsaw) while in creative states of mind.

My mom and I have a funny inside joke about that. While my studio was in her garage when I first moved to Washington State, there was no running water inside the studio. So I would go to the greenhouse just off to the side of the garage and fill a couple of water jugs to save the few seconds it takes to walk there. This makes just as much sense as finding the closest parking spot to the door at the gym. I'm extremely impatient when it comes to interruptions during a state of creative flow. Knowing this, I have to make all these provisions before I start to work. This is all fine and good, but the water pressure in the greenhouse was way too low for my patience, so I would let it slowly trickle into the jug and go back to the studio to prepare something else.

Out of nowhere, a panic-stricken yelp that sounded frighteningly close to the sound of my name would pull me back into the clutches of reality and my mom would be standing at the door of my studio with her mouth gaped open and a "What were you thinking??!!" look strewn across her dumbfounded demeanor. The garage would be flooded and my face would flush with embarrassment as I landed once again on terra firma from Planet Creative. I wasn't...thinking.

So now, whenever I drift into space, we laugh and cite the funny explanation that covers all bases, "Shut the water off, Colleen."

I am obviously not a master of the art, but multi-tasking is definitely ingrained into my insatiable desire to do everything that my heart desires as well as the things I absolutely have to do in this short but sweet little period of time that we call life. I became a master at trying to fit the fun things into the "work" equation. This can be a good thing as long as no danger is involved. Scuba diving and sculpting at the same time can result in losing track of your buddy and your depth. As any good, rule-abiding scuba diver knows, this can result in death. That's bad. But it was really fun trying. Driving and dreaming is not a good combo either. I had to find a happy medium and learn when to draw the line.

"Do not try this at home. Your bathtub is too small."

The Dark Side of Escape

When escape becomes an addiction, this is when the lights go dim and the party is coming to an end. I can remember when the first escape that led to addiction happened. Escape came easy to me. Being an artist... this goes with the territory. Escape becomes an addiction when there is pain involved; when it is too dark to come out of the light we have created, whether through a drug or a polypeptide produced chemical that takes us into the comfortable alter-reality inside the inner sanctums of our minds manifesting as everything from self-pity to control issues.

I was sixteen when I was raped. That's hard for me to say even now, and there's no easy way to sneak up on saying that one. I never called it a rape when it happened, and wouldn't for another ten years.

To me, it was my fault. I had already fallen in love with the effects of alcohol and had drank more than my share at a high school party. Alcohol affects judgment. It makes a great excuse for saying and doing whatever you want. I can remember flirting with the guy in the corner, but then the stage went black. When I came out of the blackout, it was too late. There was so much alcohol pumping through my system that I felt like I was inside a dream. I wanted to scream, but it wouldn't make it past my thoughts. I could barely make out that there were people walking through the room to use the bathroom as the whole thing was happening. That night, I somehow made it to my friend's car, and I rode home with her as if nothing had happened.

Up until this point, I was a fairly confident and friendly person at school. There were no real cliques to me. I greeted everyone with the same jovial inner light. I never felt alone. But the world looked different that following Monday. People were whispering and looking at me funny. One of the really pretty and popular cheerleaders that I had always thought of as being so cool bumped my shoulder as she passed by me in the hallway. An ugly sneer wiped the pretty off her face as she shot her hate through me with just one word. "Slut." She turned and snickered to the other cheerleader and seemed to skip off into a sunset as my heart shattered, shot from my chest, bleeding across the floor.

She was right, I thought to myself. It was my fault. I should have never allowed myself to get so out of control. The bubbles left me that day, and an overwhelming darkness crept into the corners of my mind. The innocence was gone. I had experienced something I now wanted to bury, and drinking became the deep rich black soil that could cover up every ounce of pain.

Before this, I had experienced a few jolts that could have just as easily started me on the addiction path a lot sooner. Fortunately, they didn't seem to affect me as negatively as they could have. My parents were divorced when I was twelve, a minor setback or hiccup in today's modern world. However, it was a little less common when and where I was growing up. We'd grown up along the side of a golf course that my grandpa had built from a cow pasture in the quaint little town of Massillon, Ohio. I had three younger brothers at the time. The very youngest was only a year old. Divorce was already a fear hidden in the recesses of my mind because it had happened to a friend of mine. I remember waking up from a nightmare about it once. My dad came to check on me and I made him promise to never leave. We never saw it coming. My parents didn't fight. On the surface we were a perfect family...

A year after my dad moved out, my mom decided to move back home to her parents' house in Washington State. We went from a big three bedroom home with plenty of room to run...snowmobiles, mini-bikes, my own pony; a princess's life... to living with our grandparents and eventually, a little one bedroom shack.

We left Ohio in the flying colors of the excitement painted by the strength of my mom's spirit and the promise of an adventure in a brand new world. Even the first sight of the great mountain called Rainier was thought to be a really cool cloud formation to a car filled with curious kids from the flatlands of Ohio.

At that age, little did I know of the strength my mother had when she made that decision. Four kids, a dog and four parakeets all piled into a Chevy Citation to head out west in the dead of winter. We planned to make it to my aunt's house in Helvetia, Oregon by Christmas. Acts of God carried us on golden angel wings throughout that trip.

It was one of the worst season of storms ever that year. We had blizzards chasing us the entire trip. At one point, our engine almost froze in the four degrees below zero temperatures, but miracle after miracle seemed to keep us truckin' right along. I learned a lot about how to deal with the troubles in life on that trip. No matter how scary it got, I can remember my mother's smile, her laughter, and her happy-go-lucky attitude. Her motto was basically, "what won't kill us will only make us stronger." When another obstacle came up, she would just smile and say, "Well I guess God is preparing us for something REALLY great." That's the way she saw it. Trouble was just an opportunity to learn how to get over the next hurdle, to clear a path for something new, and to gain strength in the art of escape.

When we were running out of gas in the middle of the Midwestern United States with a blizzard the size of Texas on our tail, and no sign of gas any time soon…we sang at the top of our lungs. Grateful for where we were, and that we were headed somewhere. Looking back, she must have been scared off her rocker, but she just sang, and when a gas station finally appeared, a huge sigh of relief escaped as the car sputtered to a stop in front of the pump. My mother's faith was infallible. I watched miracle after miracle unfold on that trip. I believe now, that this then was a foundation for hope that carried me out of many moments of darkness looming in my not so distant future.

Moving to a new town is never easy and I went through the typical adjustments of a girl my age. My mom worked as a waitress and my brother and I had paper routes to pay for any of the extras we wanted. We always had what we needed. My mom was always grateful whatever the circumstances.

One particular Thanksgiving that I can recall, we found a couple of grocery bags of food on our doorstep. The charity that my mom had donated some cans of food for needy families, somehow figured out that we were one of the needy ones. I will never forget, nor take for granted, the Thanksgiving tears streaming down the humbled cheeks of one of the most gracious women I know. My mother didn't share much worry with us. We only found out after the problem was fixed. Over the years every tiny miracle, from having the exact change from her tips to cover the bills to smiling through the scary explanation that she needed to have a cancerous growth in her uterus removed, mom never showed any lack of appreciation for each and every gift from heaven above.

Danny

The first summer we went back to Ohio to visit my dad was exciting. I couldn't wait to go "home." My dad had moved back into our house until he could sell it. When we drove up the driveway all of the "Kimmensville kids" came up to see us.

We lived on Kimmens Rd. There was a sign at the beginning of our mile-long country drive that read "Kimmensville Population 12 ½" This was how many kids lived on our street. The fraction was there because my youngest brother, Joe, was still on his way when the sign was made. My cousins lived next door to us, and the rest of the Kimmensville clan were just part of the gang—a lot like the "Little Rascals" TV show that I grew up with. I even named my Shetland pony after my favorite character on the show, Darla.

Danny was the same age as me and we were inseparable from the second time we met. We'd moved from Chicago when I was about two years old. A year previous to the move, we came to Ohio on vacation.

I had very round cheeks and these must've made Danny curious, so he scratched at them, perhaps to see if they'd pop. For the rest of our stay there, I hid behind my mother's legs, but just before we left, enough courage had been bestowed on me to knock him on his keister. When I showed up a year later, I'd earned some respect and we immediately became fast friends.

I've never been one to back down when a good challenge presents itself. Grade school had separated Danny and me to some degree. The difference between boys and girls was starting to set in and Danny was destined for Catholic school while I remained public domain.

I'd noticed one boy in particular in those early days at Moffit Heights Elementary, but he didn't seem to notice me at all. He rode my bus too. One day, as I was getting off the school bus, he suddenly seemed to see me for the first time. I shyly smiled and blushed and turned away, daydreaming that I was Darla from the "Little Rascals" and that any minute he would burst into song to let me know how much he cared. My stop was coming up and I knew I'd have to pass him. The beats of my heart shot from my chest and seemed to make the ride even bumpier with their resounding echoes. I rose to my feet in almost a wobble – totally bedazzled by this magical moment, and as I passed him by, his face turned into an ugly grimace. He stared straight into my eyes, and said, "You are the ugliest girl on this bus!"

I don't remember crying or telling anyone about this. Instead, I sunk into my imaginary world where wild creatures come alive and there in the dark, I emerged a different little girl. I was no longer the curly haired "chipmunk cheeks" they all knew. I was "Cat woman". I sank deeper into my role over the next week or so, even finding some thorns in a rose bush at the corner of the playground that fit snugly beneath my fingernails to form "purrrrfect" claws. Then one day, when my once crush—now turned crusher, rounded the corner of a big rock that was plenty large enough to hide behind, I surprised him with my super snarly cat growl and hiss. My claws grazed his arm, and in a panic he ran. He never bothered me again!

Thereafter, I became great friends with many of the picked-on kids over the years. A soft place in heart had been opened for them. Together, we learned to ignore the bullies and their cruel natures. What I know now, is that the cruelty that seems to fester inside certain kids is more a manifestation of their own insecurities and they are more afraid than most of the kids they pick on. I learned this as an art teacher in the inner city schools of Pittsburgh.

After school and in the warmth of Ohio's summers, Kimmensville was my haven. We built a semblance of a tree house consisting of a few boards nailed to a tree down in the apple orchard that sat on the golf course. My Grandpa Black had built the Elms Golf Course. The houses that lined Kimmens Road were backed by the course, which is still owned by family. It gave us miles of playground extending from our back yards. It provided our own private softball diamond until angry golfers would shout, "Hey you kids...Get off the golf course!!" When an Ohio thunderstorm would barrel through the rolling green hills of perfectly manicured grass and trees, pools of water deep enough to swim in would quickly form and disappear making it a wondrous gigantic slip and slide. We even opened up our own business selling golf balls at the green by our houses. The balls were retrieved either from the ones lost by golfers in the pond just a hop, skip and free fall run from our houses or by Reagan. Reagan was one of the neighborhood dogs that would sit on the edge of the yard and watch for stray toys to magically bounce in or out of peripheral view. This was kid heaven and remains as my "happy place" whenever I need to drop into one to this very day.

Upon returning that summer after having moved to Washington, some things had changed. Danny had a five o'clock shadow and his voice had dropped. He'd become rather handsome. After a quick hello, I couldn't wait to see my friends, so I hurried inside our house to call them all and make our summer plans. I had written to them the whole six months I was away.

Time slots filled quickly, and soon my stay was almost over. One of the last days I was there, as I was on my way out the door and across the golf course, I heard Danny's holler from his back porch, "Hey Keener (his nickname for me), whatcha doin'?" I was on my way to my friend's house to go to a horse show and in quite a hurry, so I explained myself in a short skip of a stop and then continued the run. My girlfriend was letting me ride one of her horses in a barrel racing competition. A favorite pastime that I'd picked up on with Nellie, my second horse after Darla. I was excited to get there.

I don't recall much about the show that day. On my way home, as I passed Danny's house, I thought of stopping to see what he was up to. He'd seemed somehow strange when I had to quickly stop to see him earlier that afternoon. But I smelled like a horse, so I hurried past to go clean up. Just out of the shower, another friend called to discuss what Danny was doing. He had apparently become quite popular at school, and since he was my next door neighbor AND cousin, I was suddenly popular too.

I walked to the window with my hair wrapped in a towel to look over to his house. There was an ambulance in the driveway. With the accuracy of a fourteen year-olds perspective, I immediately came to the conclusion that this must be my aunt or uncle and they must've had a heart attack because they were old. They were in their forties... (I'm that age now, and for some reason it doesn't quite seem as old as it did then). I yelled to my dad and he ran out the door to go see what was going on.

It seemed like it had been forever when he finally returned. I didn't have to ask what had happened. His face was pale and sallow. I'll never forget what he said. It hit me like a ton of bricks that fell from the top of Mt. Everest. "Colleen... Danny shot himself."

I suddenly froze inside a wall of time. My blood turned to icy little pin-pricks and time stopped. A million questions entered my mind, all centering on fixing the situation. "Is he okay?" was all that I can remember saying back. It must've echoed through my mind for the next hour and possibly even that whole following week. It is amazing how fast our systems kick into gear to get everything back into working order when a traumatic situation hits. Danny was not okay. He survived on life support for one week after the traumatic shot to his head. It was no accident, although I always wanted to believe that he would have called it one.

I sometimes would look back in the ensuing years wondering how I did not fall after that devastating blow to my childhood "wonder years". Instead, I was on a crusade. In speech class, I wrote a paper and spoke of Danny's suicide in an attempt to save anyone caught in an abyss of depression and who might be considering such a tragic escape.

Never in a gazillion years would I have ever imagined that I would travel the same road.

I had my first glass of vodka and orange juice when I was fifteen. I had moved back to Ohio to live with my dad for a short period of time the year following Danny's death. In this first sip of alcohol there was about 10% orange juice. My cousin made it too strong by accident and had told me to take a big sip of it so she could add orange juice to make the mix more proportional. Well, in my mind that WAS the proper proportional mix!

That first sip was the warmest, most inviting swarm of yum barreling down the inner workings of my chest that I could ever remember. I know now that this is not a normal reaction to so much alcohol. Despite this, I didn't dive into the escape. There was nothing in my life to escape from. As time passed, getting drunk became a way for me to socialize and eventually, when the traumatic seemed unreasonably inescapable, alcohol was a slow descent down the rabbit hole of a long, drawn out, self-torturing attempt at suicide.

On a beautiful sunny day in Washington State, the gigantic evergreens that line the blue skies with majestic power can bring even the most oblivious passersby to their knees. It can be breathtakingly beautiful. I could not imagine never seeing them again.

I had not gone to school that day and as I drove down the road towards my house with all the plans set in motion, I said goodbye to the trees. I said goodbye to the birds. I was never going to see them again because I planned to die. Any amount of trauma can completely devastate the life of a teenager. Between the rape and the ridicule from the kids at school, feeling intensely misunderstood, and my horrid luck in the realm of boy-meets-girl world, I thought that life was over at the ripe know-it-all age of seventeen.

I took twenty-seven prescription Benadryl pills and had a backup plan if that didn't work. When the pills seemed to have no effect, I went to the garage to start my car, but to my utter dismay, my mom's car was in there. I can barely remember trying to push her car out and mine in. I wanted to die in my own car, but there were too many people hiding in the bushes outside that night. Let alone the cartoon raccoons that kept snickering at me through my peripheral vision. Luckily my mother's window was right outside the garage so when I revved up the engine, she came out to see what was going on. It didn't take her long to notice that I was not in the correct frame of mind, so I was driven to the hospital and forced to drink some black stuff to rid my stomach of its contents. When I woke up, a policeman was there, explaining that I was lucky he did not arrest me. Suicide was against the law in state of Washington.

My mother barreled through counseling with me and survived the next year or so until she happily sent me off to live with my dad in Florida for a while.

Many attempts to escape life followed. Most were spent inside a bottle. Over my last year in Pittsburgh, I was seeing no sign of hope and no end to the perils that came with nasty drinker's dragon breath.

Lifelight

I looked forward to the happy hour of each day when I could laugh and watch the Ellen DeGeneres show. In a last ditch effort to appease an aching destiny that still yearned for my return, I sent a painting to her in care of her show. I spent my last $450 to crate and ship the 5'x6' painting. My passion to create art was slowly dwindling through my fingertips. I had lost the desire to paint and sculpt.

I was slowly dying and yet, I knew that I wasn't supposed to. I knew I was supposed to help people. Many years before this, an angel had whispered this on a part of my heart that doesn't die. Ellen did great things for wonderful people and the painting I was sending her carried the message of this hope in an angel I had painted, who had heard the warning of the storm on the horizon, but like me, was oblivious as to what she should do about it.

I had equipped her with rainbows for wings, reminiscent of the angel I experienced. Far behind her, storms raged in the skies. Inside her sweet naivety, she had positioned herself just above the serene waters of a pond and was testing them with the tip of her toe to ponder the thought of a plunge.

All around her there are warnings. A merman is plunging into the air above with a gasp of pending threat. This was to represent the countless friends who'd come far beyond their comfort zones to help me along the way. I painted a wise old woman who is the wind whispering in her ear to just use her wings… fly away. The trees behind her are hand-stretching out to grab her and pull her into the darkness. Under the water a mermaid screams to jealously hold back the merman from warning her.

I'd encountered jealous behavior both in myself and in many others and seen the ugly side of what can hold us back. Even the reflection in the water of the hideous storm behind her seems to be sheepishly warning her of the evil twin brother. In the foreground there's a Praying Mantis licking his lips over a juicy ladybug.

The whole painting is painted in a strange "off" perspective to give it a dreamy, wavy, otherworldly feel. I called the painting "Lifelight" to illustrate the nightlights… the little warnings we don't see in life that scream for us to fly away on the rainbow wings that are our gifts.

On this wing of hope, I sent away my angelic reminder of destiny, hoping perhaps that on the wings of another angel, she could still spread her message of hope, because mine was leaving me.

"Life-flight"—4'10"x 6' Oil Painting"

Chapter 8
BURNT MARSHMALLOWS

I love burnt marshmallows... maybe more now in life than ever. I've never been the best in the kitchen. My mind gets so focused on other things that cooking something to eat seems like a waste of time to me. I enjoy good food, highly appreciate the art, but would rather be elsewhere. This could have trickled down from my impatience at the campfire and contributed to a lifetime of distractions that have given me a taste for anything charbroiled. I've even burnt water! Seriously. I left some boiling one day and wandered off—only to be reminded by the familiar smell of burnt pan. Charcoal has almost become a staple food for me. In my competitive ice-sculpting days some Russian ice carvers cued me in on this great secret cure for vodka hangovers. Charcoal. Straight up. No ice.

While writing this book, my best friend Christine called me one day. She was, to say the least, a little frazzled. After a few colorful explanations she burst right into what had just happened to her. My mouth dropped, memories of past experiences flooded my thoughts, and I listened as she explained the unfolding of events.

It started out just like any other day would. Her brother-in-law in Hawaii had called to let her know that her sister needed her. He told her to get over to the house immediately. Without any further explanation, my friend was on it.

Christine and I met in High school. She sat in front of me my sophomore year in photography class. On the first day, the teacher announced our first assignment. He was going to take a picture of each of us and we would learn the art of developing film from this first negative. As his lens pulled up to each and every face smiles were recorded; shy, nervous, sometimes demure, each student wanted to make a good first impression, but not my Chrissy. A larger than life tongue spilled out of the little devious grin she'd had since the first announcement of this project. Her big brown eyes rolled so far back into her head that I swear she got a glimpse of her very own mind at work! I knew then, we were destined to be friends. She brightened my days in high school, and the more I learned about my new friend, the closer we became. She was not from the happy-go-lucky side of the fence. Life had already served her lots of mud pie and she was eating it with every bit of sweet satisfaction that the best of a chocolate cheesecake imagination could muster. She was a true survivor.

When Christine arrived at her sister's, she found her shaken and extremely disturbed. She led Christine to her bathroom. It was soaked in what she later described as more blood than a horror movie, the aftermath of her sister's friend's suicide. The main artery had been completely severed. All the investigation work had been done and everything to save her had taken place.

Without further need of explanation, Chris sent her sister to chill out with the neighbors, grabbed a pair of gloves and some bleach and just started cleaning. She had it all under control. Not an ounce of emotion pierced through the thick skin that had developed over the years, and when something finally did get through, it was more of a bewildered attempt to understand her lack of empathy. Everyone else seemed to have plenty. Why had she been able to calmly fly through this like she was wearing a superhero's cape—covering it with such grace and honor, leaving her sister feeling as safe and as normal as she'd had the capacity to in that moment? She'd even cracked jokes through the chaos. When she called me the next day after a healthy night of sleep, she wondered if she had just lost it. Why was she so cold? Had she lost her sense of compassion?

She explained how she felt cold and disconnected from the whole scene. Her sister's friend was an addict. She'd been in a fight with her boyfriend and was staying with the kind-hearted sister for a few days to get it together and sort things out.

Recollections of my own experiences washed back up onto the pristine shores of my mind and the oily residue glistened its light of reflection on my charbroiled past. A cute little marshmallow appeared on the beach and raised its weary head smiling at me like one of the little minions from the movie "Despicable Me". It was blacker than my last name and an old familiar smell of charcoal whispered sweet melodies of the campfire songs that scared away the boogie men haunting the thick dark forest of my past.

The day that my cousin Danny committed suicide with a bullet through his brain began just like any other day. I didn't cry when I'd heard the news. I felt awkward and out of tune. I had stepped right into autopilot and functioned in some highly tuned robotic fashion. When the dam of tears finally burst a week later, that reaction seemed so cold in reflection.

There are many ways to cook a good marshmallow. If you're patient and careful, with a steady hand, you can hold it in the coals just right—slowly cooking the inside to a softened melted perfection and a caramel coated crust that adds exquisite flavor to any s'more. These are the well-balanced, soft shelled species. They fall apart easily, smoosh nicely into position and are the ones most likely to please the general public.

The fast-paced, impatiently cooked marshmallows are thrust into the flames with no pretense or deliberation. They are simply thrown onto the stick and burnt to a crisp, leaving the inside cold and spongy. Somehow, I found myself relating to these charred marshmallows. Chrissy is a charred one as well. We are used to being thrown in and out of the fire without being cooked.

Huge tidal waves and forces of change do not faze us much. Flash burns calm our perspectives. We adapt quickly and actually function normally in situations that should threaten our sanity. In fact, we end up shining like compressed charcoal and it's the slow, methodical cooking that freaks the little charred ones out.

This is what diamonds are made of. My cousin Ronda Fisher wrote a book called *"Multifaceted and Fabulous,"* in which she beautifully correlates the pressures of women's lives to the nature of diamonds. Over time, and with enough of the right kind of pressure, we can reflect the light of one situation into a spectrum of beautiful color and turn what was once a dark, cold, seemingly bleak situation into a rainbow of possibility. In order to capture this spectrum inside what lies at the end of every rainbow, it is vitally important to see behind the black of your present situation, and realize your destiny. Life operates on a brand new color frequency when you see the crystals in the charred ruins of the wars you've found yourself thrust into and inherently know that ashes are not the end. There isn't an end. Beyond the black of night, diamonds appear in the sky as sparkling reminders of an infinite beauty. I have a deep and sensitive curiosity that wants to soak in every ounce of nature I can plunge my soul into and reflect it back through a work of art, if only to inspire every little charred marshmallow on the planet into a realization of whom we REALLY are and what our true purpose has every possibility of being.

Chapter 9

AN ARTIST'S EDUCATION

Curious

I always felt a connection with the stories behind other artist's struggles. Whether it was Van Gogh, with his passion that will live on forever inside the swirls of starry nights, or Michelangelo and his courage to stand strong against the powerful Catholic Church and be true to his vision that went so much further than the vision of the times. Jackson Pollock's struggle with alcohol touched me in obvious ways, but Lee Krasner's devotion to him and her respect for his genius to thrive gave me goose bumps.

Artists all have stories. Personally, I believe that every person graced with life on this planet has a tale to tell and inside their auto-biography is a hidden treasure just waiting for the right moment to blossom. I've always been attracted to the guts, the real side, the inside story. I want to dig deep and find out where the seed is, how it got there and where it has traveled to land on such a fertile or infertile soil of soul.

What really makes us tick? This is part of the reason I am writing this book. I'm curious. I want know. And the more I let open the door of creativity to write, the more creativity comes in. The universe was born from creativity and I love feeling its breeze whispering across the spongy corners of my thoughts.

I've always been curious and its roots have had to grow and struggle through a lot of rocky regions to take hold of this young artist and give me a drive like nobody's business. If someone told me it couldn't be done, I've always felt challenged to prove that it could.

I can remember being taken into the hallway after an Algebra 3 exam and asked to describe how I came up with an answer. When I explained how, my teacher gave me a baffled look and said, "Well, I've never seen it done that way, but your answer is right." It's not something that I am particularly proud of, but it's never been easy for me to follow a prescribed path or take direction from others. This has been a blessing and a curse for obvious reasons. Those who follow a well-worn path are much less likely to get hurt, have struggles, or be wrong. I was wrong a lot. To top it off, I have a stubborn Norwegian nature. Which is kind of an "Oops, I'm wrong. So what? Next hurdle please." It's certainly made life fun.

From my earliest days, I learned to turn to the spark of creativity for the answers my curiosity was searching for. This gives rise to an extremely active imagination and coupled with my desire to find truth, makes for an interesting combination. Growing up, I loved to explore. Some of my best memories were of finding pretty rocks and looking into their geology, which lead to their history, the planet's history and ultimately every kid's fascination… dinosaurs! Inside the rooms of museums my mind wandered and pondered and the more it did, the more I wanted to learn. These were the earliest memories of self-teaching. It started with a burning desire to know what was unknown. This same desire has burned throughout my life and has escalated through my art.

Every chance I had to explore, to try a new avenue, was taken. I learned to face fear head on and to love it. Growing up with three brothers and my cousin Danny was an awesome addition to my adventurous nature. With all the boys around, I never got too far into the world of Barbies. With their influence, I turned more towards mini-bikes, snowmobiling or driving fast over the rolling hills of Massillon, Ohio in my dad's Corvette.

I was just a kindergartener when I got Darla, my Shetland pony. She was a stubborn little thing. I loved racing her across the pasture pretending to be shopping for the castle's needs. I was the princess and our shed, the castle. Danny and I used to ride her up the long dirt road we lived on to a farmhouse that always seemed to have chocolate chip cookies. Danny sent me to do the asking. This would be advantageous later in life when I had to sell encyclopedias door-to-door to earn spending money.

Odd Jobs

Although I never lasted long in the "real job world," I always kept a strong work ethic, as long as it was doing my art, that is. If I strayed too far from art, or was not working towards the goal of making art in some fashion, every bone in my body quickly grew uncomfortable. I couldn't last a month unless I could convince myself that this was forwarding my art career. This mindset or focus is not as hard as it sounds if you have the right attitude.

For instance, once I had to take a job cleaning toilets for my ex in the bathrooms of his restaurant/nightclub. Instead of being bitterly angry, self-righteous and ticked-off that after accomplishing so much in life I had to stoop so low... I sang. Empty bathrooms are confidence boosters. If you sing loud enough, anyone can sound like a rock star. I sang, laughed and bolstered my confidence level, thanking my ex, God and every lucky star that I had this job to lift me out of the s*** hole that I'd found myself in.

The jobs that rang out loud warning sirens through the marrow hallways of my bones were the ones that others looked at as possible careers. I knew my career at the age of two. No matter how far down the dark tunnels of life I would venture, I always knew where home was.

Adjusting to working and living in the real world became an art in itself for me and my family. After my parents divorced, we learned the true meaning of struggle and hard work, though even before that I had worked as a paper delivery girl in Ohio. I got my first ink in a newspaper as "The Pony Express" when the paper I work for found out I delivered them on my horse. My part Appaloosa, part Mustang—with a mane that would never rest across her neck—gave her a permanent Mohawk. She had a tail that had lost most of its hair from twirling like a helicopter when she was excited, which was always. I used to barrel race her in the local horse shows. We took home a lot of blue ribbons, either because she really was super quick, or her looks scared the bejeebers out of the other horses. Together Nellie and I set our sights on beating my brother Tom, who shared the route. He usually won. I always got stuck sweeping up "road apples". I didn't really give a flying funk-o-meter. Competition was never a major drive. My motivator has always been curiosity.

My art teachers all throughout my elementary and high school years were wonderful and supportive, but I didn't start to get all wacky with my work until high school. Up until then, I had always been fine with the puppies, kittens, rainbows and scenery paintings. After our move to Washington state and the devastating blow of Danny's suicide, my high school art teacher helped me to start using my drawing skills as an emotional outlet.

Mr. Bitonio was the savior of my sanity. He seemed to understand in a way that only another artist could. He introduced me to the world of Salvador Dali and I lost myself deep inside that wondrous tunnel of forbidden art. My very first step outside the "normal paintings" box was a fish with a human eyeball. I wondered what the fish saw staring back at me through the fishbowl, so I covered one eye of the oscar with a bubble and drew a human eye in it. Mr. Bitonio always had cool assignments that sparked the imagination, but most of all, he was down to earth and real. He cared about each and every one of us and showed it with genuine concern. My high school years were rough in many ways, but I kept it hidden from the general crowd. Mr. B read straight through it, and knew just how to mend my broken pieces. All it took was a pencil and some paper.

After high school I worked at Burger King for a while. I then decided to move to Florida. My dad was going to help me through technical school to become a design artist. There seems to be a stigma in this country that making art is not a real job and that artists are generally poor and starving, so I thought I had to find a way to support my ever-growing need to create. Design art would not prove to be the answer. Technical drawing class put a worse taste in my mouth than moldy, disgusting, dry, stale toast after a three year hike through the desert. I felt like a foot stuck in a glove and I don't think I even made it through the semester at this school.

Bored to the brim with waterfalls of drool, my interests turned to a boy. He was a bad boy. He didn't like class either, and had this bright idea about selling drugs to earn fast money instead of having to work hard. I had not been exposed to hard drugs up until this point in life and the thought of them, and the people that used them, scared me. But who was I to judge…? This naivety and lack of discerning consequences to stay away from sketchy situations, lead to a very stupid decision. I continued to hang out with this good-looking boy, despite his bad-looking choice in occupations and because I was present during one of his dealings, I ended up in jail for a night and on two years of probation. I was too freaked out to say anything when a pile of money was thrown in my lap and I was asked to count it. The "Welcome Back Kotter"-looking undercover police officer looked like he could rip my head off with one slice of an evil-eyelash, so I quietly did what I was told and this made me an accessory to a crime.

Blessings come in odd packages. I then got a job as a grocery store clerk. Only a few months passed when my personality as a jovial "grocery food flinger into the bag" person was about to land me the high ranking award of "clerk of the month". Being on probation means that you are special. You get a list of rules that most of the rest of the world has not earned the right to abide by. One of these special people rules is that you have to report your crime to your employer. Well, my little "mightier than thou attitude" was that I wouldn't have gotten the darn job in the first place, so I failed to mention my prior indiscretion. I had a very pro-active probation officer that decided this was not acceptable and in a surprise visit, he was instrumental in the first time I was ever fired from a job. My heart sank. If I couldn't keep a job at freaking grocery store, how was I supposed to work? AH-HA... my art! I would show that no-good, pompous probation officer. I decided to work for myself. I would not fire myself if he told on me. Ha-ha in the system's face, and into the world I now love with every bit of passion that I could muster up I zoomed. I became a freelance artist.

My first job was to paint a mobile dog grooming van. I covered this van from front to back with dogs of all shapes and sizes doing dog things. Peeing on tires, licking each other, sniffing butts. It was a mobile hit. The owner was extremely happy and paid me well, and we even got press coverage.

Eventually I did end up having to supplement my income, so I worked a few more odd jobs. I fitted tuxedos at the mall, became an architect for two weeks until they asked me if I had actually earned a degree in art school. I never lied. And there was a sly smile on the head architects face when he let me go. All things in life can stack to your advantage if you just put your mind to it. Everything from my jail time to begging for cookies with my cousin has been instrumental in my world of art. The longest stretch of working for someone else while I lived in Florida for two short years, was my job as a clerk at an art store. And at least there, I could get a good discount on what I really longed to do for a living.

A Love for Books Nearly Got Me Shot

At age 20, my brother Tom, who lived with my dad in Florida as well, decided to move back to Washington with mom. We missed real grass. Florida crab grass is pointy. My cousin sold us his Datsun B210 for $250 and I painted all the rust spots with gremlins eating away at the car. I got a little carried away and eventually they covered the car. Our drive across the country was beyond adventure. Because of my paint job and my brother's ferret who needed to be exercised regularly at rest stops, we met many fun and interesting strangers. One trucker escorted us across the Badlands and even let us take turns riding in his cab so we could see the reflection of the sunrise stretch across his refrigerated trailer! It was a beautiful sight that I will never forget.

We surprised my mom with our arrival and I soon found a job selling encyclopedias door to door. My love for books and genuine love of people helped in making me lots of money in short amounts of time. My boss wanted me to become some big shot in this field, but I just wanted to make enough money to paint. I worked as little as possible and spent most of what I earned on art supplies. While working my magic in the field one evening, I came across a particularly handsome book reader. He didn't buy any books, but I ended up following him back to his hometown in Ohio when he left the military.

In Ohio, that place I thought I would never move back to, I found another book-selling job. Ohio was great growing up in, but I didn't think it had much to offer as far as the world of art goes (wrong again).

My new encyclopedia company did not pay half as well as the one back in Tacoma. They had a much stricter credit rating and would end up turning down over half my potential buyers. In Tacoma, we had a military base which was guaranteed income and granted automatic credit approval. Ohio's employment base did not grant me this luxury.

On one occasion I was even chased out of a house with a pistol pointed my direction. I had two appointments that evening. One was in a questionable section of town so another sales rep volunteered to come with me. She had done quite well with the company and had just bought herself a new Lincoln Continental. We decided to take her car instead of my old beat down Honda Civic.

When we got to the appointment, a humble young woman in an apron invited me into the kitchen to show her the sales presentation. I started my regular rap. About half way through, my partner started to tap my leg under the table. At first I thought I must've forgotten something so I began to take my time, get a little more thorough. The taps increased and even started to hurt. When I finally looked into her eyes, a terror was written over the once pretty blonde smile, so I kicked it up a notch or five even further.

At this point, the small-framed housewife seemed very nervous and by the time we were ready to leave, a very angry and slightly drunk husband was waiting for us. Unbeknownst to me, he had been pacing back and forth behind me in the living room guzzling down beers and muttering nonsensical banter about the new car in his driveway and the "no good, money-thieving, book sale swindlers about to steal their hard earned cash" for some books. Pistol in hand, he let us know in no uncertain terms as we scurried out the door, to never return despite his sweet, mousy, little wife's desperate plea to the contrary. She wanted them for her kids, and it was one of those moments where if I could have given them to her...I would have. After a few months of sparse paychecks and plenty of sales experience in the field, I decided it was time to get a job where I could stay in one place. A sales clerk position in an art store became available and this job turned into one of the greatest ventures in the education of my artistic life.

Art Store Clerk University (ASCU)

Multicraft Art Supplies was a small, family-owned business. My boss was a musician in a blues band and the other two employees were painters. Not your average artists either. Carrie Lewis was the assistant manager. At the time, she was at the end of her career as a full-time mom. Her kids were grown and she was getting back to her amazing talent as a landscape artist. Michael Musgrave was my co-worker. His talent goes beyond words. His story is a book in itself and he became my best friend.

Michael later introduced me to Jack Richard, who became my fourth private art instructor. The first was my Aunt Viola, who'd found my passion while I was still a child. She died much too young and before I could even get a second chance to paint long hours into the night with her. After her passing my parents found a painting class near my hometown of Massillon that I went to on Saturdays with my cousin Lisa.

After moving to Washington, I took lessons from a beautiful lady named Marjorie Mankin. I always appreciated her encouragement and warm smile.

By the time I took lessons from Jack, I was full of blank pages and readily soaked in his vast knowledge like a dry sponge to water. Jack is a renowned portrait painter and an amazing teacher. He has had a great influence on my work, even to this day, I can hear his voice and advice every once in a while in those times when I seem to need it most. I learned the art of color from him, the importance of light, the free-willed sweetness of what it truly means to do what you love; the love of good quality paints and brushes, and so much more that it could be another book. Although Jack was not a sculptor, my first sculpture came from a class with him.

Jack told me a story once about the biggest portrait in the world. He was commissioned to complete it. It was a portrait of Theodore Roosevelt done on the pavement of a park in Washington DC. The only way to view it was going to be from the sky in a helicopter. He was commissioned to design the layout of the colors, somewhat like a paint-by-number composition. The sidewalk was then divided up among people who would purchase a square. They then proceeded to draw their block of color with chalk.

Jack, being the innovative and savvy artist that he was, knew how the politics worked. So after the plans for the project were complete and handed in, Jack disappeared until it was too late to change anything.

He had the most infectious smile when he told me this story. He then went on to say that most people want to have a say in a commissioned piece. They will find something wrong, and want you to change it, even if it is dead-on perfect, they will feel much closer and surer of their painting if they have a part in it. It makes sense and is all well and good, I thought. He then went on to tell me a beautiful secret. He said ... "So, if you don't want to change anything, paint the nose a little off, or something else that you know they will spot. Then when it comes time to view the painting, either you will help them find it or they will, and everyone's happy."

Jack is a true artist. He paints from the soul no doubt. He used to have art history lessons along with slide shows once in a while. They were nowhere near the art history you'd think would put you to sleep on a Monday morning, no way. Jack knew the real dirt. He told us the soap opera madness behind the paintings that popped up on the screen and always with that sly smile and infectious laugh, because deep down he had it too. These are the kinds of little life lessons that I find so important to learn every once in a while. To this day, Jack gets thought of more often than he'll ever know.

In between Jack's classes and working at the art store, I learned and took advice. We had every kind of customer there, from art student, to college professor, to the professional. We carried top quality paints, thanks to Carrie's and Mike's influence, who were students of Jack's as well. Over the three years at the store, I learned to decipher good advice from bad. But, I'll be honest, it was rough in the beginning.

Bad advice came in different shapes and sizes. When the college professor told me my work was too literal, it said too much and was too illustration-like... it was like hearing that girls are too girly. I knew deep down that I could never change. My art would always have a story behind it. Now that I'm older, I see what he was saying from a different light. My art WAS very illustration-oriented. An artist has to learn technique through a series of basics. FUNdamentals are the building blocks to fun. Until I learned every tweak of a muscle fiber, the link to every bone and the way they dance across our anatomy, I could not be free enough to dance with my paints. This took what seems like forever, and I am still learning, of course, but oh, how I wish I would have known this in my younger years when I was so sensitive to criticism.

Behind the Mask

The first time I let my art be on display at the art store was a nightmare. I displayed a colored pencil drawing called "Behind the Mask". It was a clown who was scratching the paint from his face. Two of his fingers were growing claws on them and a tear washed some of the makeup off as well. I drew steps across the painting because I had a very imaginative kitten who had decided to chase an invisible mouse across my unfinished artwork and left claw marks on the paper. The steps were melting as they ascended and the icy blue was becoming molten orange. In the clawed hands a puppet melted onto the steps and a green essence formed footsteps ascending into the lava. The clown's hair became ribbons with hidden faces and even a money sign. Bubbles were the last addition, my peace of mind... and now for the translation.

I was a confused and torn teenager when I started that picture. I worked on it over a period of years. The clown was me. I felt like I had to wear some sort of happy face, a fake smile to please everyone. People tend to scatter in chaos... hmm...go figure. I didn't want to wear a mask anymore. I wanted to take it off, but felt trapped and feared that I would only get hurt if I did. (This is the reason for the self-mutilating claws) I felt somewhat exposed... which is the puppet exposing my self-mutilation. In hindsight, my early drinking days may have had some influence. This burning desire to just "be" was melting the cover (the green envy puppet) onto my path.

I knew I was in a cold state. I was young and even though young people think like they know it all, deep down we know better. We know the years will melt the covers. We hope they will warm our cold and lonely feelings deep down, so desperate for the acceptance of others. It was also reflective of yin and yang. The good is always mirrored in this life by a dark side. It is how we choose to walk through these periods of life that allow which side prevails and takes influence.

Inside a bubble in the lower right corner is a picture of me in a dress catching a frog. As mentioned in a previous chapter, I love frogs. Frog songs are peaceful. Lord knows I've kissed my share of them and they are loathed by so many. I guess I have high hopes that my love for them will somehow balance out the hatred. Danny and I used to escape to a pond that was in the middle of the golf course we grew up on. There were hundreds of little tiny baby frogs around a particular time of year and we loved to catch them. The bubbles are the fond memories that carry me away to a time of innocence, wonder, excitement, and bliss.

In the ribbons are the voices in my head that were whispering lies and telling me that I had to please the crowd, do as I'm told, and be a puppet. "Get a real job or at least paint pretty pictures people will buy; not these weird ones" the voices would say. Two giant hands seemed to umbrella over the sunshine of my soul keeping the "truth light" from shining in. And finally, a money sign in the upper left. I was broke. People kept telling me I should be rich from my art and I wasn't. This didn't settle well with me and left me angry with my circumstances.

"Behind the Mask"—32"x 29" colored pencil"

Obviously, I was quite close to this drawing. Putting it on display was like ripping open my chest and allowing the next person who happened to walk by to perform open heart surgery. But I did it anyway, and in walked a lady with a bun so tight she could barely blink. Her husband tagged along behind her in a trail of dust from her determined walk. I forget what she was looking for, but she asked me in a way that demanded I get it for her and that I was to be her little slave monkey for the next several minutes of her valuable time.

I led her and her husband across the floor toward her desired product, which happened to take us directly past my beloved clown. I didn't stop, but heard her strong footsteps come to a screeching halt. Her voice still sounds like the wicked witch of the west in my head, and as I turned, I heard her hiss, "OH what a TERRIBLE picture! This is horrid! Who would display such sickness...?"

I think this went on, but something soft made of self-preservation must've blocked out the rest. I could feel the ground shake and a waterfall of tears welled up in my throat. She kept ranting as I kept trying to lead her to her product. Her husband may have noticed because after a raised eyebrow glance in my direction, he started to try to rush her along. She was oblivious though, and just continued with her vitriol. I wasn't alone in the store with them. When Michael saw them coming he recognized the attitude that came with the bun type and suddenly needed a smoke break. Mike had overheard the entire episode, but didn't emerge until they were almost done. There was nothing he could do at this point except watch. As I rang them out, the biggest explosion of tears was on the verge of bursting that I think I have ever had to hold. When the bell on the door signaled that they were finally gone, Niagara Falls had nothing on me.

Huge lesson in that. Not everyone is going to understand or like your art. Be prepared, understanding and empathetic. I am grateful to this woman today. She taught me how to keep my mouth shut and gave me a deeper appreciation for other art that I may not have ever looked at before. I now look deeper into everyone's work and have respect for their space and their heart. To me, this woman became an angel that taught me such an important lesson about life. Now... if I can just remember that when I encounter the next pea brain that cuts me off in traffic...

Lots of great advice came from the little art store. Students were always a joy, even the ones that hated art class or were only there because they had to be to get their degree in rocket science. I would get every detail I could about the class. What projects they were doing, what were the requirements, why they had to do it and then I would pick and choose which ones would fit what I wanted to learn. I would work on the same projects they were, but with my own end game, to help me learn anatomy in the way I wanted, or make a color wheel to adjust to what I needed for my own home studio. I even went as far as to sneak into some of the student's classes. I could not afford to go to college, but it did not mean that I couldn't get an education from one. Professors generally did not mind at all. As a matter of fact, they were very happy to have a student who was there for no other reason than to learn. I even took a few lessons in a music appreciation course that gave me insight to the lives of musicians and the way that they paint pictures with notes. Many paintings and sculptures carry an influence from those classes, even to this day, and I'm sure they will till I croak.

These were the days of my self-education. I would go to the bookstores with Mike after work and find countless anatomy books, medical journals and art books. We set up shop in my basement and spent our time painting, drawing, laughing, and talking about the heart and soul of art itself.

One of the books I found great interest in was by Kimon Nicolaides, called, "The Natural Way to Draw". The lessons in that book are intense and brought about a dramatic change in my art. I would wake up at 5a.m. to catch the earliest bus to work so that I had at least a few hours to draw and to write in the morning before work began. During this time, I also read Julia Cameron's excellent book on finding your inner artist called "The Artist's Way," which started a writer's streak in me. Nicolaides' book however, was transformative. It teaches gesture drawings, which taught me to dance with figures, and blind contour, which gave me sight. The mind tends to skip details when an overall picture is the goal, but an artist needs to learn to notice them. Artists also need to feel the movement in what they do… feel the movement of the wind in hair, the drip in a bead of sweat on a hot day, and the passion of foreplay when intensity rises as anticipation of seeing a long lost lover for one last rendezvous nears. All of these considerations play into an artist's keyboard and floats through their hot, pulsating bloodstream as the notes flow like blood and milk spilled onto a canvas forming a moment in time. All to only be awakened by a single viewer who simply will not leave until this moment is purchased and hanging on their wall, forever placing them there…in just a passing moment….in just a glance, a work of art is a portal.

Chapter 10
SCULPTURE

Playing the Market

My life in the world of art began with painting and drawing. It was not until my late twenties that I even considered becoming a sculptor. In fact my first encounter, besides the soap I had used to carve in the bathroom to pass time, was to use one as a model for a painting. I was painting a bull and a bear in an open field fighting. It was a commission that my dad wanted done for his office. He was working as a stockbroker in Florida at the time. I was studying under Jack Richard, and when I couldn't find a good picture of the two in the right position with the right lighting, Jack suggested sculpting them. So I did.

It was the first time I had seriously sat down to sculpt. I didn't know at the time that in a few years I would be entering the world of bronze and ice, stone, mud and even scuba-sculpting. I had been a full-blooded painter up until then, feeling only the rush of paint through my veins. I wanted both the bull and bear to be in full motion doing what they do best at "market value", with the bear slashing his great claws down and the bull slicing his horns up to an unknown outcome. The risk of the stock market, separated by a river of numbers—the codes that give us a clue as to what the businesses are doing with our investments. When I picked up the clay, I never questioned whether or not I could do it. I don't think that little worry has ever been much of a question. I don't mind giving anything a fair try. I am not made for cheerleading, line dancing, or anything consisting of set patterns in large groups, this is for sure. But I've given them all a good try.

I can remember having this "I can do anything if I just put my mind to it" kind of drive when I was really little. I was completely convinced that I could fly. When my mother told me that this wasn't possible, I got very frustrated. That night I had the dream. I dreamt that I was coming outside to fly. I'd been in this dream before and had flown many times with great success. I did what I had always done. I ran as fast as I could across the back yard and then out onto the open plains of the golf course... the wind lifted my arms up into the blue...but something was different. A new heaviness had entered the scene and I knew that this would end my magic powers. The weight of doubt was just too much. It did its dirty deed. I haven't been able to fly since, but I learned a very important lesson. We all possess this magic ability to accomplish and create the unknown, unseen, impossible things in life. This painting gave me a boost of confidence, allowing me to take a chance at something new. Coincidentally, this is the way a lot of people view the market, and it makes me smile funny when I look at it now. To think that the stock market brought me to where I am today with sculpture in such an unconventional way makes for yet another one of those "imagine that..." moments.

"Bull and Bear"—28"x 22" oil painting

Magical Pink Clay

After the painting of the bull and bear, I didn't really think too much more about sculpture. It hadn't yet grabbed hold of me like an out of control circus animal yearning to experience the wild outdoors.

Then along came Mick. Mick was a mild mannered construction worker at the time that used to come into the art store to buy polymer clay. He was always very friendly and polite, and soon became a friend to Mike and me. One day we noticed that Mick was digging a little deep into his pockets to find the money for this expensive clay. Mick had a dream. He was going to go to Hollywood to sculpt monsters for the movies. We'd never seen anything that Mick was working on, but thought it was a nice dream. One of those chain craft stores was opening down the road from us. And although they were taking much of our business and eventually would be the cause of our beloved family-owned art store's closing, we told him that they sold the clay for another 40 percent off. He thanked us profusely and happily disappeared for quite a while.

The next time we caught a sight of Mick, he was dressed a little different. He wasn't wearing construction worker clothes. He looked like he was sporting some brand new shiny shoes and wore a smile to match. He marched into the store and I called to Mike to come and see our long lost friend as I watched him approach across the parking lot through our giant front window.

Mike and I had become inseparable friends. He loved art as much as I did and his father was a very accomplished watercolor artist, so Mike had a wealth of information about the art world there in Akron, Ohio. He and I went to art lessons at Jack's together, always had a ton of fun working together, and kept each other perpetually inspired.

By the time the sparkly new Mick rolled up to the counter, Mike and I were waiting for him just inside to say hello. We'd missed him. We did not expect to hear what he was about to tell us. "Hello guys," his mild manners were like sunshine compared to some of the cloudy demands of other less appreciative customers, "I just wanted to come back here, and say thank you."

We listened, "Because of your recommendation, I was able to buy a lot more clay. So I made a lot more monsters." At this, I could feel my heart sink a little. By that time we were facing news that the big chain store was running us out of town with its ample ability to buy in bulk and offer huge discounts. A sign of the times.

"A company in California that I have been applying to be a sculptor for was impressed with how many sculptures I had made and I am now off to Hollywood to make monsters for the movies." Mick finished this with a smile that sent a gleam of bright light off his teeth.

Our jaws dropped. Lots of people have dreams and some make big goals. But very few work hard and long enough and diligently enough to accomplish them. We were witnessing the beginnings of a superstar and it was exciting. We'd never even seen any of his work, so the questions rolled out like the sound of frantic little mice scurrying around a gigantic brick of cheese. We wanted to know everything.

Mick went on to tell us of this amazing quest he was about to embark upon and eventually invited us over to see his monsters. The work was like nothing I'd ever seen. Mick had painstakingly sculpted every sinew of muscle and bulging protrusion of vein necessary to complete the hideous horrific look of a full blown monster in a small scaled model. He was a huge fan of Ray Harryhausen, creator of a form of stop motion model animation known as "Dynamation". "Clash of the Titans" and "Jason and the Argonauts" were a few of his claims to fame. Mick had the ability to go as far as he wanted with his intense love and knowledge of these monsters and their makers.

His enthusiasm about the clay he used inspired both Mike and I to pick up a pack of it for ourselves. After a few weeks, I finally pulled out the clay and began twisting it into a form. In this moment a magic entered into the mix and as my fingers pushed the pink colored clay to the sound of "In Your Eyes" by Peter Gabriel.

To my surprise, I watched this lump of pink plastic clay transform itself into the belly of a woman. My hands fell into place as if I was experiencing a déjà vu, only I was not. I felt the feeling of being at home in this new land that had only been waiting for me to pick up the tools, recite the magic words and click my heels three times. I watched in mysterious awe as my hands performed like beautifully trained masters in a dance. A tear escaped and several more followed and I was in love. I couldn't put it down until I was almost finished. It came as quickly and as easily as my first brush stroke and the first story I ever wrote. I felt this rush of warmth come over me and I needed more clay. Immediately.

The weeks that followed turned into obsession. I was ready to sell some paints just to get my grubby little mitts on more clay. As luck would have it though, I was a clerk in an art store that gave us a fantastic discount. Sad as it was, the store happened to be going out of business. So the sales that followed in those next few months devoured all of my paychecks. I had a very gracious live-in boyfriend at the time who was not very happy about this once he found out that his cooking job was to be our sole income way before I was even losing my job. Thanks to him, I did not have to sell any paint. (Some of the tubes of paint I bought and still buy were $60 a tube. They've gone up since then.) I bought more, in fact. I stocked up on everything I could. None of us knew what we would be doing to support ourselves once the art store went under. But for some strange reason, I didn't worry.

The clay I used to sculpt my very first figure was incredibly forgiving. It stayed pliable for months, held its shape perfectly, and could be used over anything that could withstand 170 degree heat when it baked in the home oven. At any point, it could be baked then carved and sanded, pieces ripped off and new ones sculpted into place, then re-baked again re-sanded and over and over until finished. A person could not go wrong. I could not stop talking about it. This clay that used to collect dust was now constantly on backorder.

The Fall

My first figure was fast and furious. A story unfolded around her, just like it did so many countless times before when a painting would take me to the far off regions of Never-neverland. The way that her body bent backwards gave her the feel of falling weightlessly to some unknown fate. My mind picked up the story right there.

Ohio was always spectacular in the fall with its rolling hills and miles of deciduous trees to light up the cool, crisp days with colors bright enough to outshine Christmas. She became a love story that even today, seems to echo through the empty corridors of my mind. She became the season and took on the life of one of its leaves. I created a man to catch her and called him Winter. I pictured the change of seasons almost like the changing of the guards, or the way relay runners hand off their batons in races. They would only touch for a moment, but live next to each other for an eternity. Far away and so close, a deep love would bind them, but nature would separate them forever.

Like the leaf on a tree, her colors changed as a passion grew inside her in sweet anticipation. With each day that hid the subtle kiss of briskness in the air she longed for the single moment when fall meets winter. The warm red and golden glow that replaces the friskiness of green and the passing of an adolescent summer would soon consume her. Then, filled to the brim with excitement, one last breath heaves her away from her life-sustaining family tree and she falls weightlessly into the arms of winter as a deep sleep forces her to lose her gaze into the icy blue heat of his eyes. Winter lovingly covers her with his soft blanket of snow, longing for the day that she would wake up in his arms, but it never comes. Inside the dark corridor of dreams, her warm glow sinks through the earth and fills the roots of the trees with the soft lullabies of the musical season of spring.

The cold longing and loneliness of winter's icy tears slowly begin to melt away and a new hope restores youth throughout the land. In a boyish glory that brings excitement and adventure soaring through the branches of trees in sweet sonnets of windswept love songs, he calls for summer to wake up. The sound of her name in the warm air of spring tickles her branches with a promise of sunshine that sinks to the very roots of her soul. Her sweet young innocence playfully pushes through the tree in tiny yellow buds of spring and the cycles of life begin once more.

"The Fall" my first figurative sculpture. About 10" in size each.

Chainsaws and Ice

The seasons are a beautiful love song filled with the rhythm of life and pulsating through our veins. Cold harsh winters are always replaced with the new vitality of spring. I believe seasons are a part of life that we can use to build a depth of character otherwise dulled by lack of experience. Some of us have weathered through unfathomable storms with threats of time coming to a stop in the depth of winter's demise. Deep within our roots we know this too shall pass. In that moment is the awakening of the spring, and the fullness of summer soon to follow.

Winter is a wonderland filled with adventure. Snowmobiling across hill-enforced drifts that I am positive are specifically designed for catching some air, this season is ripe for adventure. And with some guidance from some gourmet sauce entrepreneurs, another glory was just about to catch my drift and whisk me away to downtown "Passionville". This was the ultra-cool world of ice sculpture.

With the ever-encroaching end to the glory days as an art clerk nearing an end, all of us were looking for new places of employment. I had picked up some side work from a company who'd come to our establishment looking for an artist to do some paintings of chefs as backdrops for their displays. Because they had happened along at just the right time, they had heard of my exciting new venture into the world of sculpture. So they offered a recommendation to try ice as a medium. Ice carving is a chef's trade. And as explained in the chapter about burnt marshmallows, I am no chef. They told me the name of a professor that taught this art form at the University of Akron. He was a chef, so I assumed that I would need some expertise in that area. The idea went away as fast as it came.

Chef Alford, who simply preferred to be called "Chef", was another of our rare and wondrous customers that visited our little art supply mecca. One day he brought in a plastic golf travel suitcase filled with chisels and other strange tools, most of them power tools. He was looking for something to fit in the case that I can't even recall. When I asked him what he did with those tools, he was happy to tell me all about it and I was so happy to listen.

He told me he taught ice at the university and I put two and two together. I joyously recited my love for the new-found world of sculpture, and he invited me to try sculpting ice with him at the local ice manufacturing plant. We set up a time and I skipped off to the backroom to find Mike and tell him about the upcoming adventure.

I told him about all the travel Chef had spoken about. He took his ice carving team to Mexico, Jamaica, and various places all over the states to compete in sculpting competitions. I have to admit, it was the travel talk that sparked my rear into gear at first. Michael listened patiently, as he always did. Then he brought up things that should have worried me. Ice carvers use chain saws and other power tools to work as fast as possible with their ever-changing medium. I hadn't really thought of this.

"A chainsaw on ice. Hmmm...." his deep voice recalled from my explanation, "what if it kicks back? You could cut your head off. And is it electric? That's dangerous you know... mixing electricity and water..." Mike had a great point. But I'd already committed to giving it a try, and Chef had even offered to pay me for the sculptures if I could do well enough.

The moment the chainsaw hit the ice, I just knew. A chainsaw slips through ice like a hot knife to butter. No kicking back to interrupt me on that point, and rubber boots solve the electric shock possibility. The rest of the world faded to black all around me and I fell deep inside the crystal chasms that shot out of the shower of snow as the purr from the chainsaw's motor locked me into a trance. Each and every power tool became an extension of my arm. I was well on my way to becoming a tool junky at the first bite they took into the frozen crystals of my dreams.

Sculpting ice is intense. This was taken at a world ice competition in Lubeck Germany... she had something in her eye.

I traveled the world on this ice cube. I had to sign up for a full semester at the university in order to be on the ice team, so I actively sought out financial aid and was off to college in no time. The carvings for local weddings and parties that Chef had hired me to do paid enough supplemental income to keep me rolling. Lucky for me, I didn't have to take any cooking classes to be on the ice team either, so I signed up for all the art courses that had interested me back when I was sneaking in to school to learn art.

At this point I had been to many places around the country and visited Canada twice, but had never had use for a passport. I was very happy to change that. At first, I started off with the local competitions. If they were far enough away, competitors had the option of carving a sponsor block. This was an ice sculpture that was paid for by a local business and in return we had our hotel stay paid for. That particular

Valentine's Day, there was a competition in Medina, Ohio. I signed up for the sponsor block with romantic intentions.

Bloody Valentine

My boyfriend Matt, whom I had met trying to sell encyclopedias to back in Washington was working full time and going to school. For quite a while, I had been feeling a tension growing between us. I rarely talked to him even though we had been living together for five years. He was always studying, so I happily stayed out of his way and kept busy with my art. My best friend Mike moved into the apartment below us, so I spent most of my time with him, naively unaware of how this felt to him. On our limited budget, I thought a nice suite in a hotel with a hot tub would give us a chance to talk. So before I left, I wrote a note with my concerns spelled out in an ultimatum sort of way. I had high hopes of a beautiful and romantic rekindling that Valentine's Day.

When no phone calls came to my room and there was no sign of him, I choked back my fear and called him. He wanted to end our relationship and had held off telling me this for months now. He sounded relieved. I fell to pieces. When it came time for me to carve the sponsor block, I was a wreck. I explained what had happened to Chef. What he told me next hit me like a bug chasing the pretty lights on a freeway. I had expected sympathy and an excuse to go home. But Chef Alford knew something about me that I had forgotten. Like any great coach, he knew his team members well. He knew what made our hearts spin and drove us to reach our maximum potential, and he also knew that this too shall pass.

So with a pat on the back and a warm sympathetic look of fatherly wisdom, I sniffed off to carve my sponsor block for the local newspaper. A warm bath in a wintery Alaska is no comparison to what happened inside those few hours. All was forgotten. I left the scene of the accident and entered the joyous land of "Colleen world". There was no pain there, only intense concentration and the beauty of the little paperboy delivering his news.

The next day at the competition I could not wait to start sculpting. My thoughts were playing a game of darts on my heart and the only thing to stop them was a wall of ice.

Ice competitions are set up like a race. Although we are all in competition with each other, there is a sweet camaraderie amongst the ice carvers themselves. We are all racing with the ice and the elements surrounding us. Light turns ice into chards no matter how cold it is, so most of the serious carvers have tents to shade the sculpture while it is being built. Below freezing weather of course is preferred and unless you are in a refrigerated arena, this is not always an option.

Competitions are set up with judging criteria that is fairly standard, especially in NICA (National Ice Carvers Association) sanctioned events. This included things like usage of ice, which is how well you could utilize the material you are given inside the 10"x20"x40" standard block of ice. In order to make the best of this limited block of ice it should be well thought out beforehand. So an ice sculptor prepares for a competition weeks ahead of time, designing a 3 dimensional puzzle that sometimes... well, most times, is dependent on precise cuts so as not to distort the other neighboring pieces. Ice carvers use templates to transfer the design onto the block. If you ever notice little black marker lines on a hotel's walls, you can be fairly positive that your hotel room housed an ice carver. We use a projector to enlarge our drawings onto a 20"x40" newsprint template that we tape to the wall with masking tape. In my own experience, many of the carvers were full-time chefs, creative geniuses in their own rights, and would decide to either change the design at the last minute or would still be working on it the night before. In our hasty attempts to do this, the marker often makes its way off the edges of our templates.

Another of the categories judges how far you dare to take the ice outside the block. Once your ice is sliced gingerly into its pieces, there is a freezing technique that started with marble slabs and graduated to aluminum in the midst of my carving days. The smooth surface and heat conducting ability that marble or aluminum slabs offers is used to melt a surface into a perfectly smooth and flat one. We use an iron to heat the slabs. Sometimes a freezer box is used to make the ice cold enough to freeze two flat surfaces of ice together simply by pouring a little water between the two. Dry ice helps a lot in any of the freezing techniques.

I did not have a partner that day. Having a partner is a preferred and highly recommended option in competitions, but in some ways, I was happy to be on my own. Partners can help do anything but put tools to ice. When working with a 300 lb. medium like ice, anything can happen, and I was about to find out just how helpful asking a partner to help would have been. With the whistle blown, the buzz of more than twenty chainsaws broke the stillness of the air on that crisp February morning. Once again I was lost in my own little world. All seemed to be ticking by like precise clockwork. It was a beautiful day, and despite my lack of sleep, I felt good. I was prepared and as ready as I could be to compete that day. My template in place, I began to separate the block with the sweet sounding whirr of my favorite tool. As I rounded off a corner, a tall shard of ice slowly started to tip away from the block. My left hand still holding the saw, I quickly reached over it to catch the vital puzzle piece before it split to smithereens in front of my bloodshot eyes. The saw tipped on its fulcrum with just enough power still turning the razor sharp teeth to tear through my right glove that had just saved the day.

I felt something strange under the ripped material. But it didn't hurt so I didn't want to look at it. I was in the ZONE. Against better judgment, I decided to ignore the weird feeling in my wrist. I kept carving.

Just as my mind had forgotten all about what had happened only seconds before, a scream erupted from the crowd outside my tent. I looked up to find the source of this startling commotion pointing at me. A little annoyed at this interruption, I looked down at my wrist and took off the torn glove. This next part may get a little gross for the squeamish, so skip the next paragraph if that's you.

I had never watched real tendons move and work with such precision. It was actually quite beautiful. There was very little blood, I had just missed a main artery. The screams around me seemed very far away and I was still very peaceful, lost inside this new view of flesh and bone.

Then snap! Back to reality! Someone grabbed my arm and thrust it into the air. Before I knew it I was riding inside the back of the ambulance, bawling like a newborn baby. And then laughing because I was not at all phased by the tragic incident that everyone thought I was crying over. I was heartbroken on Valentine's Day, and had slit my wrist... on accident.

Nineteen stitches later, I arrived home to a very sympathetic, but not sympathetic enough to change his mind, ex-boyfriend. Neither of us were in the position to get a place on our own, so we decided to stay roommates until one of us could. This sucked despite his accommodating mannerisms and helpful attitude. It hurt way too much to have to look at him every day. My mission soon became to travel, as much, and as often as humanly possible. This was luckily, very feasible in the world of ice.

No Plans, Just Travel

My first adventure was helping teach ice and other culinary art at a university in Guadalajara, Mexico. Chef Alford had also been teaching me the art of tallow. Back in dinosaur days, they used to use butter or beef fat to sculpt displays for buffet tables. Nowadays a paraffin based wax has replaced the traditional tallow. It is much easier to work with and does not melt in the sun like butter or attract flies like rotting beef fat. This wax was a lot like my first clay, and I soon found the medium as natural as slime on a slug. I traveled with Chef and other talented culinary artists to Jamaica, and various parts of the USA to sculpt in all kinds of competitions and teaching opportunities. One of the perks of this lifestyle was an obvious one. I no longer could call myself a starving artist.

News traveled of popular acclaim with the help of Chef Alford, and soon I began to venture off on my own. I spent lots of time in Jamaica, and even helped with the grand opening of the Sandals resort in Turks and Caicos.

I had the opportunity to bring along a guest sculptor to help me so I chose my best friend Mike. He hadn't had as much experience with tallow as I had, but he had immense talent, and I knew we'd have fun. I would not have been able to put together such an elaborate display had it not been for his help. The day of the grand opening, we relaxed and joined the guests in an amazing array of paradisiacal dining. One of the chocolate tallow pieces of a boy riding a dolphin caught the eye of a local celebrity who was being filmed in an IMAX film about dolphins.

Dean Bernal had befriended a local rogue dolphin named JoJo and the film producers were just winding up the last of the footage about the wondrous relationship that Dean and JoJo had cultivated over the years. After JoJo was in a boating accident, Dean had helped nurse him back to health.

Before this incident, JoJo had been a nuisance to the locals. He'd developed elaborate plans to play with the people that did not always agree with what peoples' ideas of play were. Things like hiding under the docks that were used by novice skiers trying to get a grip on staying in the upright position while the boat takes off. JoJo would wait for the skis to hit the water and then bump them off. Funny as it seemed, it scared many of the guests and his longing for human companionship was bad for business.

JoJo loved Dean's attention during his sick leave away from the haunts he normally disrupted. So much so, that when he went back to work as a scuba instructor, the dolphin got the bright idea to herd in a shark. This would freak all the beginning divers out. So Dean would disrupt the class to take the dolphin and his pet shark off to play elsewhere. It was the beginning of a lifelong relationship.

We were supposed to leave soon after the grand opening, but with a little coaxing from my new-found friend, I decided to stay a week longer. In that extra week, I rode on a boat with a photographer named Bob Talbot and his film crew as they wound up the final scenes of the IMAX movie. I used to sell Bob's prints in an art store that I worked at in Florida. They were nice enough to allow me to help a little with the filming by swimming alongside of JoJo while the huge, five foot in diameter camera had to be reloaded after only ninety seconds worth of footage was shot. On the boat, the conversations with the film crew went way beyond fascinating.

Going home was beginning to be a problem and any excuse I could muster up would have sufficed. My return home this time happened to be an adventurous one.

An Act of Valor

During my short stays at home, Mike and I had stumbled across a local photographer who was happy to open his studio up for models to come in and pose while we painted or sculpted them. Since my first encounter with clay, I had not been able to put down the mud, so while other artists drew, painted and photographed models, I got dirty.

Joe Levak had an enormous studio in the top of an old school house. He was and is an extremely talented photographer, and he graciously traded his services to photograph my work for a sculpture that I did in his studio. His professional and former military status had enabled him to become the official photographer for an event put on by a school board in which former General Colin Powell was to be the speaker. The event was honoring war veterans. Specifically, Congressional Medal of Honor winners. While discussing his role in the event, the event coordinator mentioned that he needed a sculptor to design a small plaque for the Seven Congressional Medal of Honor recipients and Secretary(at the time)Colin Powell. Joe recommended me.

For obvious reasons I was quite excited at this opportunity. In a meeting, the coordinator described the plaque he had in mind. A simple eagle or some blah blah, on and on. For some strange reason I didn't hear a word he said. When his explanation came to a halt and the silent heat melted the wax on my wings, I fell from the sky in an Icarus-like dream and swept up the conversation with the idea I had seen in my vision of the sun.

This was no ordinary situation. I was sculpting for heroes who'd saved umpteen lives risking their very own to the piercing moment of staring death in its eyes and spitting in them, all for the sake of our freedom. I tried to explain the details of my vision. I wanted to show the heroism in the eyes of a soldier who's locked inside of an adrenaline rush. I pictured him grabbing his rifle to shoot straight into the direction of a shot fired within the same moment that he is rescuing a fellow soldier from a trench. I promised to return the next day with a sketch. I did. It was nowhere near the relief plaque that was first suggested. He took one look and was sold.

I was so wacky with the thrill of inspiration and the opportunity to sculpt for such honored recipients, that when asked if I could stay within the small budget and still get thirteen of these sculptures done in time for the event six months away, I just said yes. No research, no experience ever in making a mold or a limited edition, not even a blink of an eye. That was stupid. But OH man was it a trip!

Act of Valor"—28" x 16" x 16"limited edition cold pour bronze

My very first sculpture commission—it was way over the budget, way bigger, and was literally being finished on the drive out to the event. It had to be made in a material coined as "cold pour bronze" given our limited budget. The owner of the company that I bought my materials from and that helped me with the mold making process was so moved by my passion and the heroes who'd be receiving it that he donated half of the cost. Even with all those breaks, I did not make a single penny doing what took me months to do. But I would have paid eight times that amount to learn everything I had learned in that experience going to school.

On the base of the sculpture I made reliefs of each of the seven acts of valor. I'd been sent short explanations of what each hero had done to receive the honorary medal and was deeply moved to say the least. I went a little nuts on this, making up my own war stories and ending up with several more soldiers abstractly represented inside moments of heroism and forming the rocks and mud that make up the base.

When it came time for the event, my mom was so proud she flew out to attend the event with me. I finally met these men, whom I'd spent the last six months with enraptured by the extreme circumstances that had been thrown at them in the bowels of war. Their humble attitudes towards what they had done were nonetheless astonishing. I'd been humbled to tears over the courage behind that one millisecond decision to save the life of another and in some cases several others without concern for their own lives.

The eagle is a representation of the freedom our soldiers fought for. Inside its very scream are the cries heard from across the miles. No matter where we go in life our families and our homes stay within our hearts, fighting with us through the battles of lifetimes. We are never truly alone. The eagle is the beautiful reminder to the soldiers of a whole country filled with so much grace for their sacrifice.

The Cantine Clan

A portion of the sculpture was made while on a two-month tour of Jamaica. I was having a very hard time living with my ex-boyfriend. He was very cordial, but it was just strange and incredibly uncomfortable. Although I'd already shipped my belongings back to Washington with plans to move home again, I had to wait until I finished this commission to leave. There was no way out unless I could do another teaching trip. So I called the head chef of an organization on the island of Jamaica and begged for a retreat in exchange for whatever teaching or sculpture they wanted me to do. The result was fabulous. For the next two months, I spent each new week in a different all-inclusive resort, sculpting wax and ice across the hot tropical paradise island of Jamaica.

At the last resort, tired and lonely and longing for home, but feeling like I had none, I met Erik, my first daughter's father. He was carving ice for the anniversary celebration of the resort and I was making the tallow sculptures. He swept me off my feet. The same week that I returned to Ohio, I made plans to move to Pittsburgh, PA. My mom was a little miffed after spending the money to help me move out there with her, but my mind had been made up.

Life with Erik was always an adventure. Because he was a professional chef and a great ice carver to boot, we made all sorts of plans to enter into ice competitions everywhere across the globe. I would never have been able to finish the "Act of Valor" sculpture without his help. His professionalism is impeccable and the lessons learned while he and I were together are ones I will carry to my grave. Not only that, Erik Cantine has a way of making everything he does fun. The whole Cantine clan was blessed with the gift of "funlandedness". His brothers own airbrush shops on the boardwalk in Ocean City, Maryland and to this very day excitement riddles through me like a kid in a candy store just to catch sight of their smiles and genuine love for people. They are a family filled with talent and inspiration. Erik had trouble with my inspiration in the beginning.

Dating another artist was a dream come true, especially one as charismatic as Erik. In one of our first ice competitions he began to explain an idea that he had to sculpt a girl... or "hot chick" I think is how it was first explained, riding a dolphin. He went on to describe the layout and how I'd be able to do this well because of my knowledge of anatomy. At some point the circuits inside my mind started to catch fire which is probably when the contortion of my facial muscles shined through to reveal a not so pleasant misunderstanding of his direction.

Out of my mouth spilled something like, "A girl riding a dolphin???!! Why would you want to sculpt a girl riding a freakin dolphin???!!! .....WHAT does it MEAN??!!"

With my mouth still drooping in disgust, I stared frustratingly searching for an answer...and I love this about this man... he let out a bellowing laugh and instantly comprehended the misguided slam on his design. I certainly did not mean to belittle his idea, but I was not about to be involved in an art project that did not carry a message of depth and inspiration. With this realization, Erik was on the boat, fully supporting all artistic decisions made. Never again did he question or go against what plans I made. He always was, and continues to be full of belief in me.

There have been many moments that I have not felt like a part of this planet. I've been completely misunderstood, shunned and belittled. Pushed aside like a broken spoke in the wheel and replaced by shinier ones. I could not understand why. I knew the intentions I had were for greatness in this world, yet no one would listen. Instead they stared and compared shiny girls riding dolphins and how shapely their boobs were. It would have smashed me if I would not have had my companion's love and undying support.

On one of our trips to Europe, a couple stopped to say hello as they passed by at the beginning of the ice competition. This wasn't an unusual thing, but they then proceeded to tell us that they had come to the competition specifically to see our sculpture. There are a lot of very skilled sculptors in ice, and Erik and I had not been in the top rankings because I usually got lost in some part of the ice and by the time Erik snapped me back into reality, we'd lost too much time. A full ten points out of the 100 points given in most competitions had to do with the final touches. Your ice had to be clean... no snow or tool marks or blemishes. A good ten minutes to do this was safe. We were lucky if we skated by with sixty seconds to spare. So why was this couple traveling all the way from Germany to see us? The answer made my heart sigh in relief. At last someone seemed to notice... they had come for the message.

Moments like these gave me hope that maybe I was not alone in these thoughts. I was not the only sculptor there with meaning, every piece of art has something special and beautiful from each and every creator—even the girls on dolphins.

Erik Cantine and I sculpting ice for the world ice competition in Lubeck, Germany.

Having belief in someone is so huge. This was a sculpture of an angel that we did for the world ice competition in Germany 2004. Although Erik and I weren't together anymore, we tried one last competition together. Our usual rush to beat the clock left her in an unfinished state, but the message was intense. Her wings were going to be the shells of an egg she was emerging from. She was the yolk. The inspiration had come from a painting I'd done called "Eggsistence". I'd become tired of the face-values and empty conversations based on material worth. I longed for substance and an understanding through soul. This was my last attempt in the ice world at seeking light through the melting crystals and it washed away in a puddle of melted dreams.

It all started with a dream. A dream that came crashing down around me like failed ice sculptures whose structural integrity was pushed beyond its limit. I was going to be a mother. This dream was beautiful, one I'd always hoped for and longed for alongside a loving father as a happy dreamy family.

Italy

I had picked up a book called *"Drinking Lightning"* by Philip Rubinov-Jacobson, in which an artist had an angelic experience. The name alone had intrigued me for obvious reasons, but when I came across his ethereal enlightenment that echoed songs of heaven throughout his paintings, I HAD to meet him. It was way more than curiosity this time...the real reason is later explained in this book.

I learned that this visionary artist who'd written the book was teaching a seminar in Italy. At the time, I did not know how to explain why this was so important for me to do. An indescribable force was pulling me. I knew the gist of this force, but explaining it would take a lifetime of more experience and writing of this book. So I blamed it on my pregnancy. With begging and pleading that would have made a four year-old proud, I explained to Erik and everyone else who needed to know, that this was what I thought would be my last chance to study abroad. The timing couldn't have been worse. Erik's mom had been diagnosed with breast cancer and was scheduled for a mastectomy. My decision to leave and go do this at this time was taken as a slap in the face. I wish I could have explained more, but the truth was even crazier. So I stuck with the lame excuse and called home as much as I could.

I had an amazing time in Florence, Italy. I studied the Mische Technique under this visionary artist and writer, Philip Rubinov Jacobson, who'd become a kindred spirit through our shared experience in the wild wonders of painting with soul purpose behind each stroke of the brush. My trip had been way more than eventful. I was broke and four months pregnant at the time. The only reason I had been able to go was because a friend and collector had so generously helped with the costs. The seminar was a painting seminar, but I was still heavily into sculpture so I longed to see the masters' works in all the genres that covered the streets of that Renaissance city of old masters.

Oh and I did. Michelangelo's David brought on tears of reverence, and his unfinished stone pieces seemed to echo his undying passion to push the limits of what his true love and longing were. I had always been madly in love with his courage to do what he loved and depict the passionate stories from within his heart instead of following the church's request to paint priests' portraits across the ceiling as so many other cathedrals had done. His story gave me the strength to write my own, and I was now in the presence of his work.

Walking those streets and seeing his works, I fully understood then and understand his passion for sculpture even more so now. Painting is much easier to do and much more in demand. Most everyone wants to fill blank walls with something, but very few have the space or large lumps of cash for sculpture. Despite these considerations, sculpture has its own unique draw; the absolute sultriness of touch that comes with the emotional playground of riding a soft billowy cloud of seduction in the world of the three dimensional is something that is better felt than described. I'd found myself wanting to walk around the corners of paintings to see the other side at times… way before my hands had ever connected to my heart through that sweet little square of pink clay.

My classmates even surprised me with a trip to the mountains of marble in Carrera where David was "born". I was touched beyond speechlessness by their kindness. I would never have been able to afford to go there otherwise. They knew how much I had wanted to be there. I'd brought with me a suitcase stuffed with rags for clothes (not something I would recommend wearing on the fashion-conscious streets of Florence), but with the sole purpose of filling my suitcase with marble and pitching the entire lot of garbagy garments for the journey home. On my flight back, I was even lucky enough to have one of the baggage handlers look up at me while lugging my bag to the conveyor belt and ask,"Whadda you got here...rocks?"

"Yes." I replied.

Eggsistence

When I arrived home after a month of intense learning and enlightenment amongst artistic peers, Erik was different. The months following this were some of the darkest days of my life. I had always seen as a happy time, the pregnant bellies and glowing smiles of moms-to-be, but it had suddenly become dismal. Erik was so distant and I didn't know why. I won't go into detail about all that happened. People sometimes grow apart and although I had stopped drinking when I found out I was pregnant, I had caused enough mistrust to drive him away. He did not want to spend the rest of his life dealing with my lies about alcohol.

But as a result of my trip to Italy, I was carrying a brand new soul and the sheer reverence of this was overpowering enough to give me the strength to barrel through the gloom. As the five years of adventure, love, laughter and true meshing of our souls tore itself into shreds and rained confetti memories of happier times around me, emotional trauma was playing like a dying circus before my eyes.

I gathered up every ounce of peace that I could find so that my sweet baby girl, this brand new innocence that I was now to nurture, would not receive an ounce of pain that knocked so heavily on my heart's door. Any and every way of keeping me from sinking was used to do battle, except drugs and alcohol. This was and still is amazing to me to this day, because this had always been my emotional crutch, but now I was forced to face life like most of the rest of normal society does… and it worked much better and more efficiently than I ever imagined.

Soon after Mikayla was born, Erik finally left for good. We always remained friends and never once had to turn to a lawyer to work out what was very simple and easy on our own. We wanted what was best for our daughter and keep this as precedence to this day.

It had taken me years to pick up the paint brush and use the technique that I learned in Italy, simply because of the pain associated with the circumstances surrounding the trip. I suffered through a hardcore drinking binge once Erik left, that took me a little over two years to finally drag myself back into the halls of the twelve step meetings that had always saved me before.

The doors always remain open there. Repeated offenders are not shunned, just welcomed. We beat ourselves up enough inside the bowels of addictions, and to find this warm nurturing refuge amongst the tattered war grounds we have created around us is the feeding tube filled with love so desperately needed to recuperate from emotional anorexia.

One night, after six months of sobriety, I picked up my brush upon awakening from the insomnia I suffered from as a result of pent-up emotions and a painting appeared before my eyes. It took a lot longer than that of course. It was a painful memory that woke me, but it carried such a blessing that it had to be described.

I started the painting by using a technique I had learned in Italy, with splashes of color and glazes to enrich the tones and slowly recognized the shape of an egg coming through. I had been reborn into a new existence and I'd broken through the shells of my own ego to get there. With me I'd carried a new soul and held her like a new sun for a universe darkened with death and sadness. Mikayla used to wake up on mornings when the sun shined into our funky artist's loft in the Brewhouse happily singing, "It's a HAPPY day mommy!"

Some mornings were not so happy for me, panging hangovers and painful memories of stupid adventures from the previous night would haunt the rays of sunshine and darken them into rays of shadows. Mikayla's song was my sunshine. Her light carried me through the darkness just as my desire to fill her with sunshine and happiness while

I carried her. So "Eggsistence" became a painting of a mother's undying love and compassion.

Her bald head seemed to echo the tragedy that Mikayla's grandmother had gone through in battling cancer. It stripped the mother's identity leaving her bare and defenseless as hell raged on around her. This stripping of ego can only be reached when we are willing to face our worst demons head on. I had witnessed the power of this both in my own struggle to hold onto the sun through hell and in my daughter's grandmother through her battle over cancer.

There are two skulls in the painting. One is at the end of Eggsistence's reach facing her head on. Victims of a terminal illness must reach out to touch the face of death in order to have the peace of mind it takes to pull through. Death is always watching on the sidelines, the other face of death hides behind the brashness of his deadly brother waiting to attack in a moment of weakness.

The liquid core, the white of the egg is the soul. New or old, light of soul is able to traverse through in a "trans-parental glow" that I believe is passed down through generations. Love is hard to imagine in the material world of loss. True love only exists in the never ending path of light embedded in the soul.

We are carriers of light. The shape of our souls and the food we feed them will determine the pathway that light takes. The less that we feed the shell of the ego, the more food the soul receives. Intentions must be clear, pure....otherwise one can end up hard boiled. Soon, the layers of the shell get weaker. What lies on the outside is the new beginning for what lies within. Life outside the egg, outside the womb, and beyond our death-defying trials, makes up the surroundings and uncontrollable circumstances that transpire around us. The only "peace" to fit in the whole puzzle is in knowing that a creator exists and that good will always prevail. After this, the next step is a blind one. The leap of faith.

"Eggsistance"—36"x 24" oil painting

My First Bronze

I owe so much of my early years of success to Erik. His encouragement was an infinite flow of fresh spring water on the deserted days of rejection from shows and galleries.

Not only did Erik hold my frail, sensitive artist's hand through the dark days of feeling misunderstood, he also introduced me to his boss who'd heard enough about me at the time to give me a commission. This was no ordinary commission, this was to be my very first BRONZE. Oh… even that WORD make my toes curl up into a yearning desire to thrust myself into a pile of mud!

For those who are unfamiliar with the bronze sculpture process, one usually starts by sculpting the sculpture in clay. A mold is then made and in the lost wax method a wax copy is covered in a ceramic slurry. These shells are then put into a kiln. The wax melts away in the intense heat and leaves a hard shell able to withstand the hot molten bronze. When the shell is cracked away, amidst the powdery dust of its destruction, a shiny new bronze enters the world.

This was the beginning of the journey of my faith. She was my very first bronze. This story began with someone else having faith in me. I had no experience with bronze. But I did have a great friend who wanted to see me fly.

Blind faith is simple. It only takes a decision to take a step. But the first step is always the hardest. From the comforting bubble of familiarity, I sometimes find myself wanting to close my eyes and run after the initial burst. This is fun but not highly recommended.

With her arms open, her eyes closed, and freedom in her soul, I sculpted my rendition of "Blind Faith" as she takes the leap into the unknown. Her gut told her to do it and her heart drove the rest. Deep down there is a core existence that will tell everyone who searches, what decisions are right for them. Those decisions may go against every grain, every rule and all that mankind perceives as the norm...yet, you'll know what is right. Our conscience is a powerful tool in decision-making if used in accord with good intention.

In her hands I sculpted the scales of personal judgment. In order to illustrate the power of good and evil, they took on the form of a snake and a dove. The weight of what holds us back from our dreams inspired the serpent. I used my own hand for that pose and thought I would never recover. The snake is uncurling from its sneaky hiding place and stretches out to wrap around her braid... the last link to her precious mind in an attempt to distract her from freedom. If she would ever decide to hesitate in her walk, the deceiving serpent could inflict her with poisonous fear.

The other scale is filled with the light of love. A peaceful dove pulling the weight of judgment away from her and leading her into the beautiful light of purity of mind, body, and soul. Truth flies freely here and her creativity thrives in the weightless wonders of freedom.

I sculpted her braids to represent the thoughts in her mind that consistently test humanity and place boundaries on us through the measures of time. They turn to the chains that bind her... it usually is nothing but our own heads that hold us back. What will happen next is not here yet and what has happened, is gone. She exists in the present with no concept of time, so the braid that has chained her to this age of judgment is breaking. There is nothing to catch her step in this act of faith....there is only an openness, left purposely to the imagination of the viewer.

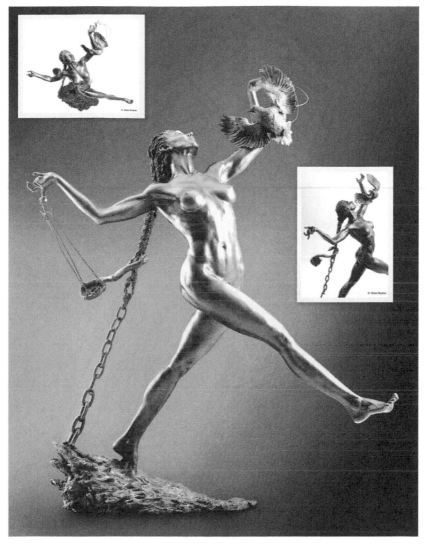

"Blind Faith"–52"x38"x48" limited edition bronze

Chapter 11
I DO BELIEVE IN FAIRIES, I DO... I DO

The Fairy Chronicles

Many moons ago—(this makes me sound so old... I've heard that Colleen is Irish for young girl, so thanks to my parents I'll never be old...) when I was in my late twenties, I had an experience.

An out of this world experience.

I was working with a good friend and fellow artist, Linda Radak, on designing a haunted Halloween hayride. We were supposedly getting paid to do this and she called me one morning to inform me that actually, we were not. She wanted me to bring my camera to where we had been working to document what we had already done.

I believe most of us are born with a natural instinct that can detect deceit, fear, or anything really, that stems from the dark side. This instinct, much like the "creativity drive", demands our respect. This small whisper is out to protect us. It usually gives us a "bad gut feeling" to begin with. Following thru on this feeling is usually, if not always, a great idea. My friend Linda was following up on hers and the usual good feeling replaced the bad one quickly when she listened. We did what we could to counteract any rebut in our pay and left the job feeling we had covered our bases as best as we knew how. I hopped into my little Chevy S-10, and barreled down the freeway towards home to get ready for a mural painting job that was giving all the artists involved freedom to do what they wanted.

I was excited to work in this way, and feeling very free. About 10 minutes after leaving Linda's house, something spectacular happened. This little moment in time has affected my life in so many ways. It has snapped me back into a purpose and reminded me that I have one when I have felt that overwhelming feeling of worthlessness that addiction can take you to.

In my Chevy S-10 there was a strip of blue on the windshield meant to block the sun's glare. On this day, however, it became a portal for a light and I'm ever so glad that its screening ability was overpowered. It all started as a spark, or a small flicker of light out of the corner of my eye. My head did not turn. I kept my eyes on the road as the light grew bigger, then suddenly morphed.

The light swirled with color and out from the color—fingers appeared, then arms and in an indescribable flash of time, I saw a being appear. She turned and her arms reached out to me as if to offer much more than a hug; more like an embrace to catch me from falling. It was strong deliberate and incredibly warm. She looked to be light years away and yet, was so close that I could have grabbed her hand. In the instant she appeared, time seemed to stop and in this same flicker of time, information streamed into my mind.

This information did not come through as words or in any other formative way that our brains usually detect new thoughts. It seemed to translate through my heart. This is very hard to describe because there is nothing on this earth to compare it to. It was like I saw into a different dimension, an emotional one.

One that spoke only heart, one that knew only love, and one that definitely knew me. She knew me closer than any friend I had ever known or could know because she knew my future and she shared it with me in an indescribable way. It was like an open book with no timeline. I could have flipped to any page and it wouldn't matter where it was, for time had no rules. My past was my present, my present was my past. She showed me links and connections to things that would be impossible in a time and space constrained world. It was so simple and so big, so complex and intricate. All laced and woven is this life we live in and it was simply beautiful.

She had a message for me. It was beyond the word sweet. It sunk deeply, straight to my core and filled me with warmth. In this emotional language that she poured through me I saw that my life had a purpose beyond what I knew, and that I must follow this creative path. I must not worry, because everything would be OK. I was covered. Tears poured over my cheeks and I couldn't understand why she was communicating all of this to me. Life was going along quite well in my opinion. I saw no sign of tidal waves in my near future. Why would I want or need to worry, and what would ever lead me to stray from this beloved path I was on in the world of art...?

There was no one else in my truck and I desperately wanted SOMEONE to see what I was seeing so through my tears of joy. I said out loud... "God, can YOU see this?" To this day, it still puts a lump in my throat. The radio scratched to a halt on whatever it was playing and the verse "I can see clearly now the rain is gone..." by Johnny Nash filled my truck cab with joy. The song continued to play and I sang it loud, laughing and crying and suddenly realizing that I was on the same spot on the freeway. I was passing under a bridge when my guardian angel first appeared and not a millisecond had passed. Time had stopped.

This kind of experience is not something easily explained to all people. It's not like I ordered a pizza and a guy dressed in a donkey suit delivered it. That one, people can accept. "I was driving down the freeway and I saw an angel," is much less acceptable. When I got home, I quickly and excitedly told my boyfriend, who duly listened and nodded. Afterwards, I soon began to doubt my own sanity. He blew it off and said it was probably one of my weird artist visions and that it all sounded like a cool fairy painting and as usual, went back to reading his book.

So I calmed down and went about my day. When I got to the mural painting job several artists were there, already lost in their worlds. We all had about a 12'x12' square to paint in this old building that was being converted into a nightclub. My friend, Linda was there who I'd seen earlier that day at our Halloween-themed adventure. Eventually artists do get hungry, so we ordered a pizza. While on the pizza break, I couldn't hold back any longer. I decided I just had to tell this story. Crazy or not. When I was about halfway through I saw Linda shedding tears. I knew it was a great story, but hadn't even gotten to the good part yet, so this threw me a little. When it was all said and done, and I had described the whole ordeal...Linda began a story of her own. Apparently 10 minutes after I left her house—which would have been the same time my experience happened, she had had one of her own. Her angel had come through her television. It was, in description, the same one that I saw. She thought she was having a flashback and blew it off, until I started to further describe my experience to her. To us, this was God's confirmation. And this addendum to the story gave me a bit of confidence that it was not just a fluke or an active imagination. This was an experience that happened outside of myself that would live to pull me from the fiery mouth of the dragon many times as the future unfolded.

Memories of my angel experience have humbly rescued me and reminded me of the truth when my mind has been filled to the brim with lies. "You are better off dead" or, "you're worthless," crazy doubts about my work, doubts that I am any good at all or that my kids would be so much better with someone else as their mother...and on and on. She came into my life at a time that I can absolutely pinpoint...a time before many whirlpools and unexpected storms, clear as day, her smile would be the warmth and the small, but clear light at the end of every dark tunnel that I was about to embark on. Her message always a reminder—a much needed walking stick keeping me from falling too far off some sort of path meant to do some good.

Fairy Dust

The special stories that follow are just a glimpse of the sparks of light that have shown up in the midst of many a dark tunnel, but usually have been followed by some sort of sparkle dust. My angel's smile is like a trumpet with violin undertones in my heart.

This first one is the most recent one. My daughter Angela's friend from Hawaii came over to the house for a sleepover. My kids, as well as other people's kids, have always been a great excuse for my actions. I get to act like a kid. This is no out of the ordinary thing for me, but at least when other kids are around I don't get strange looks. At some point, we got on the subject of fairies. Well... I happen to LOVE fairies. Ever since the angel experience, I've been obsessed with them. I always loved them as a kid too, and never doubted their existence. So I brought out the fairy arsenal. We looked at fairy pictures, read fairy stories and the girls fell asleep to a fairy movie. Before they curled up on the couch, we set up a fairy trap. The girls thought of a perfect plan. So we put fruit in a box with a lid and I rigged it so that if they pulled the string attached to the spoon, BAM. Instant fairy pet/friend.

It had been a funny couple of weeks previous to this. I had an almost sold-out show in an art opening. I had sold 30 paintings out of the 26 that were in the gallery, meaning that a few commissions had been added to the long list of sales. "At last!" my heart had let out a sigh of much needed relief, I was on my way to finally getting paid what I'd worked so hard to accomplish. In the weeks leading up to this show

I had spent the past three months in overdrive. I had been working twelve to eighteen-hour days to fill six galleries with paintings and had taken little, or no time off. I had to wake up and be in my studio by 4 a.m. if I wanted to be done for the day by 4 p.m. so that I could spend some time with my girls. A work schedule like this is somewhat rare and I worked extra hard in anticipation of a much-needed vacation that would accompany the art openings.

This particular show happened to be overseas, so in light of the success, I went shopping in Spain and Italy and I spent every cent of the measly $500 that I had in my savings account. I was happy about it. Elated...excited. It had been a long time since I hadn't had to buy used clothes. I was wearing them while I shopped in the boutiques! My girls and I now had original designer dresses from Spain. I bought my mom some fancy jewelry and a scarf. I picked up a crazy pink hat (that later turned into a painting sold to a lovely lady who accompanied me while we bought her a matching white one) and had a fabulous dinner that evening looking straight out of the gate from a day at the races.

When I got back from this amazing trip, I immediately went to work on the new commissions from the show. I usually have e-mails and sales orders all sent to me in a document form so that I don't forget any of the details of the commission pieces. Strangely though, all was silent. I heard nothing, no one was contacting me about the list that I had to do, no one called to discuss all the money I had coming, so I finally I called them.

Trouble. Everything was on hold.

The money, the commissions, every sale....ALL of it. Once again the ugly jaws of defeat seemed to be laughing in my face. My heart sank and quietly dragged itself into the ditch of defeat. Despite the news, I kept working on the commissions. I had personally talked to these customers, gotten to know them, and knew somehow, some way, something would happen to work things out. I will not go into detail of this incident, because it has since been resolved and everything worked out even better than I could have hoped for.

To top this off, in the month before the show, I found out that I would no longer be getting help with childcare assistance or help with groceries. I had needed help over the past few years to get back on my feet again. Personal triumph had prevailed. At long last, I had worked hard enough to get off of government assistance. While this was good news, it was scary. In addition to assistance, I had been living on $450 extra each month for gas and expenses and this was plenty, but now I would have to find a way to pay for daycare and groceries out of that, at least until this glitch was fixed.

The night of the sleepover, I picked up my mail at my moms and drove to daycare to pick up Angela and her friend. I was low on groceries, so we went shopping. The girls were so excited. I only had $160 left in my checking account and just could NOT deny them the ice cream, the gummies, and a few other extras. However, I also needed toilet paper and some other necessities and the bill came to $140. I caught the lump and held a tear with a grin that came when the two excited little girls started singing ice cream songs and I handed the cashier my card. I knew I wouldn't get paid till the 15th and it was only 24th day of the month previous to this... so my remaining $20 had to feed my gas tank in order to make it back and forth to work until then.

I didn't want to think about it.

Early the next morning, I woke up to excited and happy screams of joy. Apparently, some fairies had visited us that night! A tiny sprinkle of gold fairy dust on the outside of the girl's boxes was PROOF! The fairies had also eaten some of the fruit... small bites were left scattered on the floor around the boxes. It looked as though a fairy party had gone on. A sweet smile (which was actually a sly grin underneath) was thankful for the insomnia that woke me in time to help accentuate the joyous celebration of fairies and four year-old wonderment.

As they sang their little tune, "I do believe in fairies... I do... I do..." I decided to open my mail. Hidden below a few bills and some junk mail, my wonderful Aunt Judi had sent me a check for some postage to help pay for a package I had sent to her. It was way over what the actual postage was... and it was just enough to put my mind at ease.

With a lump in my throat and a sigh of relief I quietly sang along...I DO believe in fairies...I do, I do. A sweet familiar smile back at me seemed to appear in the not so distant, far-away land of the "fairies".

Many more stories have come to me on the wings of my angel throughout the years. They are small windows looking straight into heaven. I believe, much like the link I share with creativity, this special link to heaven only grows stronger with acknowledgement. I do not believe for a second that I am special in this manner. We are all given glimpses of heaven much more often than we know. As I share these stories, my hope is that you will remember some windows from your own perspective.

I also hope and pray that I never come across as "knowing" anything. I don't know jack squat about how things really work. And the more I experience, the more I realize that the amount of squat is unfathomable, incalculable, and ultimately infinite. This spins my curious little mind like a kid who's just devoured a candy store, then told to sit still in front of a door wide open to an amusement park. There's just no way I can sit here through all this. With the information age connected to our fingertips, it's easier than ever to find "things" out. But what I'm talking about goes so far beyond anything you can type or speak into a computer.

This is the link. I feel and intrinsically know it, and had a small and wonderful glimpse of it that beautiful crisp day when the angel opened heaven. We truly are connected in a way that if you think of someone close they are likely to be spurred into a thought of you and you may just get a phone call. Don't be surprised. Acknowledge it. Accept it as reality and the link grows stronger.

The scientist Rupert Sheldrake explains a more in depth view of this phenomenon and provides scientific proof to back it up. Please feel free to investigate morphic resonance. This resounding chord is the music that reverberates through emotional and biological connections. We resonate in a level so deep it vibrates on a quantum level. Inside the world of quantum physics, the world we have come to know through our physical senses becomes altogether different. Bits of energy disappear completely and reappear without the walls of time and space. Simply put, think it or better yet say it, and it becomes a resonating reality. Whether there is enough resounding energy around this spoken word or prayer or thought depends on the overall acceptance of it. The more energy there is to put the ball in motion the better your chances are.

Big Bad Wolves

When I was living in Pittsburgh, PA, a few years after my first daughter was born, there was a rather blatant discovery of the power of the spoken word. I was in the midst of a flux. I had been working steadily as a sculptor for a number of years selling a sculpture here and a painting there in galleries mainly centered in the Midwest. I was scraping by, but happy and not hungry. I had landed a job with this very excited gentleman who proclaimed to have huge accounts and contracts with Great Wolf Lodges. They were an up-and-coming enterprise at the time. Only a few existed. He was providing them with sculptures of wolves for the architecture and surrounding grounds of the resort. I was just a lone ranger artiste. The opportunity sounded fantastic. This man saw what I could do and contracted me to sculpt a giant wolf for the entrance of the resort. One wolf turned into three and because I only had about 2 months to build these 12–14 foot long giants, I called my friends Linda, Mick and Mike in on the work.

Well, none of us even thought to get a solid contract. Only when the work was finished did we then find out that this man had not even thought of one himself. So when he fell short on one of the other orders that was an optional contract deal with him, they understandably decided against his business. I have no idea if Great Wolf Lodge ever even caught a glimpse of the results of two months of grueling all night, all day work that me and my fellow sculptors did. As far as I know, these wolves still sit in a warehouse in Ohio, covered in cheap mold material.

These were the first two of the three big bad wolves we sculpted. Linda and I sculpted the two large ones and my friend Mick Wood sculpted a young wolf. My superhero friend Mike helped out where he could.

None of us were ever paid a dime. It was a tough lesson. I was living at the artist's co-op thank God, so the rent being late was to go un-reprimanded for another 3 months which would later total 6 months behind. I owe so much gratitude toward the Brew House. Their graciousness to me in allowing me time to create and to grant me a roof over my head until I COULD pay was a huge blessing to my whole career.

The wolf man claimed bankruptcy and with no contracts, we sunk. In the middle of my hound dog days I sent some pictures into one of the up-and-coming HGTV specials. They happened to love my work and enthusiasm and decided to work me into their show. At the time it was called "Crafters across America", soon to change to "That's Clever". This news kept my momentum going despite the loss. But to my demise, TV reality shows such as this one do not pay you anything. I had sent them pictures of all my sculptures, but they picked the wolf and wanted me to stick to a dog theme. My own theory is that they didn't appreciate the fact that most every other one of my sculptures was nude. Nude dogs are acceptable on TV.

It turns out that hanging dogs aren't acceptable anywhere either.

Gone to the Dogs: HGTV and the Police

I had a beautiful pit bull named Dawju, which is not some fancy foreign word with deep connotation. Nope, it simply means "dog". Mikayla was two years old when we found her and this was how she said dog. Come to think of it, I have never been a sharp one for pet names.

I had three cats while I lived there at the Brew House as well. The mother kitty started out with the clever name "Sootles" only because Erik gave it to her. She was a beautiful gray calico stray kitten born under my loft. Using her finely-tuned cat senses to the extreme, the day she was scheduled to be taken to the vet and spayed, she escaped and obviously had some fun on her own while she was away.

Following the birth of her four kittens, she slowly and lovingly had a name change to Mama Kitty. We kept her two boys and found a wonderful home for the girls. One of them was all black with a white moon on his chest. He was named Black Kitty, and I bet you'd never guess what orange tabby's name was. I used to jokingly tell people that my daughter was very lucky to have not been named "White Black Baby"

Dawju was a rescued dog from the humane society. Someone had attempted to throw her in a dumpster as a puppy. We fell in love with her at first sight and she'd become a happy addition to our family.

Pit bulls love to play tug of war. I had a Tarzan vine in my studio that hung from the 25' ceiling and served as a quicker route from my bedroom to my studio in times of need. Dawju found this to be an excellent perpetual tug of war partner and could often be caught swinging from it herself. This was always an awesome sight to behold, this four-legged queen of my jungle swinging happily in the background as I painted and sculpted in my studio on those fun-filled days on the south side of downtown Pittsburgh.

I decided this would be the perfect pose to sculpt for my up-and-coming television debut. Not only would it add a little humor, but my sweet pit bull may get some publicity as well, and help to show the world how amazingly wonderful these dogs are.

I called my friend Mike out to help me with this job because of the amount of work surrounding it and the excitement of being on TV as well. We had to sculpt the dog in stages so that the film producers could capture the whole process in one day of filming. This entailed making almost three copies of Dawju in different stages and I only had a month to put it all together. Mike was a godsend—once again swooping in for the rescue.

When the television crew arrived the day of the shoot, we'd stayed up almost the entire night before in last minute preparation. I spent all of ten minutes preparing myself, it was after all, the art and not me going on display. Because of the time crunch, I did not discover that my new sculpture was actually going to hang until the last hour before the film crew arrived. So we did the final "hanging of the dog" right there on TV. Dawju even helped pull the rope to hang the sculpture in place. I didn't envy the editors. After a full twelve hours of very regimented and set criteria, they wrapped everything up and headed for the next artist's pad.

Mike and I were still wound with excitement and stayed up half the night laughing and talking about the adventure. The next day, I decided to hit the gym and Mike thought he'd surprise me by displaying my sculpture in front of the window on the "second" floor above the mezzanine

Imagine my astonishment when I pulled up and saw a small crowd gathered on the sidewalk and pointing to my sculpture in the window! Dawju was a hit! People loved it.... Oh and I just knew they would. There is nothing more fun and delightful than a dog playing all by itself. I envisioned the crusade for pit bull justice as I ran up the steps to tell Mike all about it. When I opened the door though, his voice was low and his face was red. He reminded me of Kramer all of the sudden from the "Seinfeld" episodes when he'd done something wrong.

"Uh.... Colleen.... uh, the police were just here...." He mustered to say.

Across the street from my loft, the south side hospital sat quietly uninterrupted until this day. I looked out the window to see every blind mysteriously closed to our view. Suddenly the crowd's gaze below turned ugly and my gut just sank. The sculpture was realistic enough that it had been mistaken for a dead dog dangling suspiciously from a rope.

Instead of taking it down, we hung it on an angle to try to give the crowd below and any others affected, the relief that this was a sculpture of a dog TUGGING a rope. Simply taking it down could have caused question and maybe a few bricks through my window. By that time the news had traveled fast and spread to the gallery on the first floor below where angry people were shouting about the heinous crime committed in our building. I have to admit I was a bit proud of the people for jumping so quickly to convict the perpetrator, even though it was me and I was innocent.

After hearing how quickly news was spreading, I decided to type a letter to the hospital across the street and to the newspaper, hoping to eradicate some of the angry rumors spreading unnecessarily through the city. My dog on a rope made national news. My mom heard about it before I could even tell her myself.

Dawged out by nebby neighbors—as they'd say in the Burgh.

Years later, as I was cleaning my studio out in Tacoma, I hung the sculpture on a tree branch outside, hoping it was close enough to the road that people would see that it was not real and definitely NOT a noose.... no such luck. Police cars and the humane society graced me with visits and soon left with laughs and smiles. I'm forever grateful for the senses of humor I've encountered in the midst of getting dogged out. But this sculpture has yet to accomplish its original intent—to somehow rescue the ill fate bestowed on this breed of loving companions.

Because this is a chapter about angels, I have no doubt that they are working on this as I type. I recently had a conversation about dogs with my Grandpa Wayne, an avid dog lover whom I adopted from church. He wondered if dogs go to heaven. I told him I think they are angels sent to watch over us and remind us to stay present, love unconditionally, and take time to play. But to get back to the original story, none of this had happened yet. I had only been slammed with the reality that my three months of day in and day out work on the giant wolves was all for nothing.

Uriel, My Angel of Empathy and Grace

I needed a job. I needed one badly, but I certainly did not want to have to go back to the 9–5 working world when my big "15 minutes of fame" on TV was scheduled only two months from then. This is exactly when my ex called me and needed my help.

He was not just an ex, he was my daughter's father. And although there was some heartache and a bit of resentment that I was still holding on to, Erik had been an amazing and wonderful influence on me and had done nothing but help to further my art career. He was opening up his own restaurant and the floor seemed to be falling out from under him while the walls were caving in. I knew this feeling well.

Still, when he called in desperation that day asking me if I could come in and just help with the decor, my own walls were not looking so sturdy themselves. I knew this was going to be another freebie. He'd funded much of my bronze work throughout our relationship and I owed him for that big time. Every little selfish needy, whiny bone that lived in my body suddenly popped out of dormancy and shouted obscenities that echoed in the corners of my mind. Everything happened so fast. Before I could let what was on my mind spew from my mouth, an unconscious sweet sounding "Yes, of course Erik. I'll be there tomorrow" spilled out.

As I hung up the phone, I was incredibly angry with myself, but not really. When I got there the next day, I saw the worn down desperation and the feeling of helplessness lift from Erik just a little.

I've never been so happy to swallow my own words.

He needed help with virtually everything. He had great ideas, but had been overwhelmed with trying to do it all on the small budget that he had. Grace filled my heart. Erik had poured every bit of his all into my art the five years that we had been together. If I had even a moment of doubt, he had always been there to lift my spirits and encourage me to keep going. What I did for him was a drop in the bucket by comparison, but I was so grateful to have the chance to help. We dove right in. I painted the floors with swirling colors of fiery warmth and when figures appeared; I embellished them and then started to intentionally put them there in a Jackson Pollock-sort of style. It was a floor like no one had ever seen before. A myriad of swirling fire and figures. It got rave reviews later when the upscale restaurant was opened along with the impeccable menu. Erik was a genius of a chef and the combination of ambience and food went on to make for great success.

I had also painted some pictures for his wall and made wall sculptures to surround the dining area all in oranges, reds, and yellows bringing warmth and welcome to the underground bistro. The painting that greeted customers as they came through the door was named "Uriel".

"Uriel"—66"x62" acrylic painting"

When I painted Uriel, she was a non-stop painting. I woke up and she was there. It was 3am. So I put my camera on timer and took a shot of myself with the closest I could come to the expression in my mind. I couldn't sleep for days until she was finished. I had no idea who she was or where she had come from. All that I did know, was that Erik needed her. She was painted as a blessing, meant to warm the hearts of every single customer that walked through his doors, just as mine had been kindled by his incredible kindness throughout the years. I had never heard of the name Uriel before to the best of my knowledge, but as I stood in my bedroom loft and stared down onto the floor at the painting in progress, the name spilled from my lips. I knew she was a prayer. A hope….possibly an awakening. I looked up Uriel and found that Uriel is listed as "the light of God" and identified as the angel of repentance. My jaw dropped.

I had already painted her as an angel that takes on the pain of the world and holds a prayer in her heart knowing full well that this is the biggest of all deeds she could do for humankind. It had been just over a year since 9/11, but somehow adding a reminder to this day was just the element needed to put this beautiful gesture in motion. The post that pierces her feet is the radio tower on the top of the twin towers. Although the painting is not centered on this event, more the "aura" of it...It was the most recent representation of what she wanted to say. In the blood dripping down the spire are two drips that form the shadow of what once was. So much happens around each of us. It can seem hopeless. Hoping for one ounce of hope...and realizing that the only hope you have is to hope for hope itself. These can be moments of awakening... and realizing the whole of life.

When Uriel woke me up at 3am that night, she wanted to take on all the pain and save none for herself. Her heart is filled with true empathy. She was willing to walk through walls of fire, withstand thundering tidal waves, and endure the pain of defeat raining down from the heavens in order to help even the smallest of beings, perhaps the slimiest, smelliest, and most loathsome of toads to higher ground. Not a single smudge of judgment tainted her soul. She was pure and filled with love. I knew she had a purpose. I had no clue to the extent of this purpose, but to me, knowing that she would be watching over Erik with this in her heart was purpose enough.

I believe we all have the ability to act as this angel does. True perfection lies not in what a situation is, but in how we handle the outcome. The toughest job in life is to step up to the plate when our own plate seems full and we feel like there is nothing more for us to give. The irony in the situation is that this is exactly when our empathy can mean the most.

There were a lot of hidden extras that I left to the viewers to find. It's never up to me to tell anyone what they should see in art. I just paint or sculpt in a broken vessel state of being. Messages pour in and eventually leak out of somewhere. I hold no messages. The true message is inside one's self.

The Awakening

With the restaurant finished, and ready to open, I was now close to eviction. Erik was so grateful. He couldn't help me out completely, but offered me a job cleaning the restrooms. I took it, grateful to have a paycheck.

The days ticked by and it seemed there would be no way out. Finally, in utter lack of knowledge as to what the heck to do next, I let go. I was on the phone with my friend Michael. He asked me what it would take to save me from this crazy downhill spiral. I laughed.

"Someone would have to send me a check for five thousand dollars!" The amount flew off the top of my head. "Not only that, they'd have to offer me a job that would be forgiving enough to start after this TV show is done filming, to keep up with my bills!" I laughed again, loudly making it clear that I had come to accept this as ridiculous.

It was one of the most peaceful realizations. I was about to lose everything. After figuring out that my kids and I would still be safe, I entered the realm of acceptance. We'd had offers from friends to live with them until I could work through it. I knew that even if I ended up in a ditch somewhere, there is mud there....and I could sculpt it. I was fine. I realized that this might be a bit scary, but I would find some way to make life happy, even in extreme circumstances.

God had other plans.

I have heard something said about success not being measured by the treasure found, but by the treasure lost. HOW you recover is the measure of success.

I cannot recall how much time passed after my conversation with Michael. Perhaps an hour, but not over a day, and completely out of the blue, Dale, an old friend and collector of many of my sculptures called to see what I'd been up to. He hadn't seen anything new in the gallery he frequented and just wanted to check up on me. I gave him a quick overview, laughing the whole while at the position I'd found myself in. I jokingly asked him if I could work for him in his gasket company in Ohio. I said I would be happy to sculpt some gaskets for him, some real nice ones with some character.

I said nothing more to him. No mention of how much I owed to the Brew House... nothing. He asked if he could call me right back. I said, "Sure thing!" and hung up satisfied that I was handling this with a stellar sense of humor.

So he called back after a few minutes and what happened next absolutely floored me. He said, "Colleen, I am going to send you a check for $5000. You don't need to do anything right now, just make your TV program and we'll talk later."

A month later Dale started an art agency, paid me a salary, and commissioned me to do a sculpture for him. It was a dream come true kind of commission that every artist longs for with every commission... totally open. Basically... here's a lot of money, Colleen. Sculpt.

Sculpt I did. That was the birth of "The Awakening"—a life-sized fountain sculpture about the awakening of our spirits and souls. Hurricane Katrina had just happened and I was struck by the beauty of so many people helping one another, not to mention what had just been done for me.

Inside the base I sculpted hundreds of figures hidden in the crevices of rocks pulling each other from the mud, helping to get them back on their feet. I read Plato's "Allegory of the Cave", and the depth of its meaning seemed to interlude with the rocks in the sculpture. A story emerged inside of itself. The main figure is emerging from a rocky grave that I imagined her pulling herself from almost as if time had transformed her into a part of the earth itself. She is an old soul, meant to represent the wisdom that comes with time. Water that signifies letting go of thought falls from somewhere behind her ear and drips down her arm to her finger. Her gaze transcends beyond thoughts lost in time and into the calm abyss, the peaceful "Akasha". She is inside of a moment, embraced inside the warmth of silence.

Life gets so rocky and hard when we live inside of a fear for a future that hasn't even happened yet, or a past that keeps changing with each new justification that the ego can muster up. Wisdom and presence are the guides inside of an awakening or the "aha" moments as I have heard so eloquently stated by Oprah Winfrey. Waking up does not mean focusing on what has happened or is to happen, but what is happening right now. I'd imagined this sculpture in a beautiful garden where this state of being could easily be obtained.

The water drips from her finger down to the other palm... and she sits inside of this, inside the joy of just that moment, lost not in thought, but a loss of thought, and an awakening of her spirit. This is where freedom lives, where love flourishes and where God intended us to be. We escape from Eden every day when we dwell on thoughts that are beyond the moment that we are in.

Sculpting that piece was an adventure in itself. The circumstances that led me to the moment of her realization were another reminder of what the Angel had promised and directed my heart toward so many years before. These stories are so prevalent in my life that I could fill another book with these serendipities. Libraries are filled with them. Miracles happen in every moment. If you look for them, and catch them and thank God for every one of them, more seem to come. It's crazy fun.

"The Awakening"—56" x 48" x 46" limited edition bronze

Chapter 12
THE PORTAL: GATEWAY TO CREATIVITY

Sometimes in life, we have to make decisions that just plain suck. I personally love the power of delegation. If someone could know me so well that they could decide my meals, my schedule, what laundry goes where and maybe even what side of the bed to roll out of, I think I'd move very happily onto that magic red carpet. However, when it comes to decisions of the heart, the decision must be our own. Opinions must become just that; opinions. I have had to make decisions with no known facts to back them up, only the seed of a new dream, based strictly on the faith that it will come true.

Chose the Frog... Dumped the Prince

I was once asked to choose between work and love, though not in a literal sense. This one particular man never once flat out asked this of me, but I sensed his longing to be my everything. In the dreams of little girls and princesses and princes, this is a fairytale come true. After all, he was perfect. He was full of life and did all the fun things I wanted to do (with a sketch pad nearby or a lump of clay within my grasp). He was a

Jeep kind of guy, hiker/explorer extraordinaire. He climbed mountains and flew a hang glider, not to mention cooked better than some of the top restaurants I've eaten at. All this wrapped up in an incredibly handsome 6'5" stature. He was always on time, answered every phone call, was impeccably accountable for all his actions and was willing to do anything I asked at the drop of a hat—within reason of course. Shining through his chest was a heart of gold that never fell short when a friend was in need.

He deserved a number one position in a wonderfully perfect girl's life, and this was something that I knew deep down that I could not give him. For some, choosing between your work and the love of your life would be a no-brainer. This is true, especially if you weren't being asked to give up your career completely. But my career is not a 9–5 job. I can set those hours and specifically work those hours, but I am on the clock 24 hours-a-day, seven days a week… from the day I was born until forever. And over the months that we were together, I watched his heart plummet when I was not able to break away for the few days a month and give him and the nature around us my full attention.

What he did not understand was that if the artistic urge showed up at a time when my attention was supposed to be on him or a beautiful scene in the mountaintops, it is extremely hard for me to ignore it. This amazing man had an excellent philosophy, "No one goes to the grave wishing they would have worked more."

After much inner turmoil over this dilemma, I came to the unwelcome conclusion that I am "Miss No-one". He was perfect, but he was not my Mr. Perfect, and I had to let him fly free into the beautiful landscapes that filled his heart. My destiny was not to run off with the prince of my dreams but to hop merrily away with my creative spirit fully intact "Forever Relying On God".

A Child at Heart & An Artist's Muse

My job is different and there never was, nor will there ever be, a set timing to creativity. Much like an accident, which you can never plan for when it strikes – if you could, it would be an appointment. Creativity works the same way. It does not run on our humanistic attempts to control our destinies and has no clock. I love this about what I do. It teaches me newness in life, allows me to stop and notice the beauty in a dew drop and to be the empty pages of an open book ready for anything to happen at the drop of a hat. It also demands my respect and asks for appreciation in return. Jealously wishing always to be answered immediately, despite where I may be or what person I happen to be with. Like an impatient two year-old, it will not tolerate any amount of my ignoring its plea. Yanking heavily on my pant leg, it's often woken me out of deep sleep, or pulled me off the road, and held me in its gazing rush of sweetness—in the form of any muse it chooses to take the shape of—in order to translate the message of its passion and hope most efficiently. It is truly an honor to be caught in its grasp. If I do not rush to the easel, or clay, or write the moment down immediately, it is gone in the flash that it rode in on and I'm extremely lucky to recall fragments-if anything at all.

This is exactly the reason that a Tarzan vine was an absolute necessity to get me to my studio from my bedroom as fast as humanly possible. Whatever it takes in the future I am willing to invest… a fireman pole, super-speed chair lift, or some beam me there device from "Star Trek"— I'm in.

According to my mother, this strange little escape to a land of my own started very young. Back then, many a moment would pass when all the other kids would run out to play and there would be no sign of Colleen. My attentions were not on the softball game or the rules in the clubhouse. I was happily floating just an inch off the ground inside another plane of existence. Although I could still listen and comprehend the world around me with an accuracy that used to baffle my grade school teachers, I would live in this enchanted land as much as possible.

The lens of my mind is quickly distracted by any rhythm that sets its own beat on life. If routine is in play, I'm usually out to lunch. I'm fairly sure that there is a drug for this "malady" nowadays, but I've adapted my life and loved ones into a calm acceptance of my bipolar metronome of rhythmic existence. I quickly learned to "tune back in" when in situations where life could be at risk...like driving. This hit me hard at age sixteen. Luckily no one was ever seriously hurt in the accidents. Yes, plural. Driving is another one of those magic red carpet delegations meant for the creative mind.

The creative intelligence demands instant access; a private back door that I can enter into at any moment. It's why I end up with countless drawings on napkins, notes on church bulletins, etc. I do not want to lose any opportunity to enter the all-access door. But there is never any harshness in the demand creativity wields. This surge or rush of creative intelligence feels more like the excitement of a child at the first sight of a playground, and seems to feel neglected and will only stop "interrupting" me if I fail to give it my full attention in the moment I hear the whisper. Instant attention keeps this flow going and will ultimately kick it up a notch.

There have been times when 72 hours will have zoomed by and the only reason I would ever peel myself away from a project while in this mode was to go to the bathroom and even then, it annoyed me. Eating takes the seat of last priority. I do have to have liquid, so I fill pitchers of water and this way I don't even have to get up to go to the kitchen. It's literally that intense. Back when I used to have to work "real jobs", I have even been known to ask to take all my lunch breaks for the whole week so I could use the extended time to finish my sculpture in the backroom.

As hard core as this sounds, there is a very real possibility that it will never come back if I slip away and fail to answer, because this happened when I saw hell. It was a separation from my creative self—I actually saw a vision of a little girl with tears in her eyes leaving me, not wanting to follow me into the dark corridor that was my path ahead. I've been gone for years without creating in my darkest days of drinking, and like a lost and battered child, I had to nurture and caress my creative soul back into my life. The skills I've learned will always be there, but the beautiful, artistic and childlike piece of me, my muse, can give up on me and refuse my call. Innocence surrounds this wave of being. Therefore, I must be in that willing frame of mind in order for all the circuits to connect. It is why I cannot be drunk or disorderly in full blasts of creative heat waves. Although some of the wisdom pours through, it becomes distorted and lost.

Off the Cross

Sculpting Jesus was definitely destined to be a sculpture that was done in a clear state of mind. Around the year 2004, my dad had called from Florida and had this great idea for a sculpture. He was willing to pay the costs of having the bronze made and this always excited me. I said it earlier and I'll say it again, I love bronze. Of all the three dimensional mediums, it is the one that always says "yes". I can bend and twist limbs in any direction and balance weight like no other without the fear of losing the art in a heart wrenching crash. At the time my dad's call, I was in a time period where I'd decided that I could handle my alcohol just fine again. This was always a lie that I believed even while telling it to myself.

One thing that I found out, years after I'd finally been able to stay sober, was that alcoholics emotionally remain the age that they were when they began to blanket painful trauma with mindless thought or addiction. It was much easier to deal with life as a drunk, simply because you don't. If a bill came in the mail, it was time for a drink. The bill ended up in the trash and if I thought about it again, I needed another bottle of vodka. This coping method appears at first to work perfectly in dealing with any and all problems. It takes all of life's pressing issues right off your mind. But when you are sober for a while, these things that have piled up over the years through avoidance, added to the stupid, illusionary tricks that you've pulled WHILE drinking to forget them all, seem to have a way of rushing back.

It generally happens around the sixth and seventh month of sobriety. At once you are hit by a giant, rolling tidal wave filled with every wrong smirk, every bad business dealing, all those broken hearts...including your own, left to swirl mercilessly along a muddy wall of thought with peals of thunder rolling through your mind. This daunting tsunami is big enough to devour the small island of retreat and refuge you've worked so hard to accomplish in those first long months of sobriety. The echoing roar of guilt alone can be enough to shake the stable ground we thought we'd landed on by just abstaining from a drink. But drinking is not the problem.

Most addicts, those that may have been hiding under their "normal" guise since their tender teen years and now find themselves 30–60 years of age, have a rude awakening awaiting them. Over the years, there has more than likely been no work or progress made in this zombie zone of addiction in dealing with emotions in a mature, responsible manner. So they are now the age that they are, but with an understanding of their emotional capacity at the same depth as that of when their addictions took hold. Most likely they will deal with their emotions the same way they did when they left off. They must look quite pathetic to others when they fling themselves to the floor and scream over losses or not getting what they want. The only people who seem to have the compassion to understand this are other addicts who've dealt with this intense need for growth beyond their addictions. Without staunch empathetic support, there are many people who resort back to their addiction after six or seven months of sobriety. Until they learn to deal with emotions in a mature fashion and have the compassionate support of someone who's been there, it can be very easy to make the wrong choice. I was beginning to feel like a professional surfer of this emotional wave of fury.

Encapsulated by yet another ride inside the dust of the wild horses, my dad called and talked to me about an idea he'd had for a Jesus sculpture. I was listening, but I didn't really hear what he truly meant until years later. My mind was too blurry and lost to comprehend the beauty of what he was suggesting. I hadn't been to a church since I'd been a teenager. I was afraid of the judgment, afraid to be sober and scared to have to deal with all that I knew was crashing into pieces around me. Jesus was the last thing on my mind. I knew the stories from before and knew that he was a pretty cool guy from what I'd remembered, but every time I would start to make this sculpture, he seemed to stare back into my eyes with too much compassion and too much understanding. I would break into tears and go get a bottle of wine and sit and talk to him and cry with him, but I simply could not finish this sculpture. It was just too painful.

Years went by and Jesus gathered dust.

At long last I'd conquered a year of being sober and was riding a giant, beautifully clear wave filled with peaceful and riveting jolts of pure discovery. I was finishing the giant life-sized fountain called "The Awakening" by the middle of my second year of sobriety and was getting ready to make a trip to a Colorado foundry for the casting. My benefactor, Dale, had offered to loan me the money for some bronzes that had been left unfinished, and my eyes fell upon my dusty Jesus. Even though my dad was footing the bill for that one, it was time to finish what had been started once and for all.

He sat in the corner of my studio, untouched and a little grimy, although I had occasionally wiped the dust from his eyes to let the warmth shine through and brighten a dark moment. Jesus sat patiently to watch my every hurdle. He had been there through so much. Even before this sculpture, his presence had carried me.

I was on a schedule. "The Awakening" had to be finished for a show that was scheduled only a few months away from the cold February day that I packed up the sculptures. So with the help of my amazing hero of a friend, Michael, we left on our harrowing trip through the icy storms that seemed to just miss us until the last sixty miles of road left to the foundry. I had barely fit the huge fountain into the small U-Haul trailer and with only two inches to spare, everything seemed to be falling into place like puzzle pieces. In that last treacherous stretch, we hit a patch of black ice and jack knifed going sixty miles an hour on the freeway. As luck would have it, upon looking in the trailer in the aftermath there seemed to be no damage and we made our way south after our best attempts to catch our breath.

When everything was finally unwrapped at the mold maker's studio, we found a small amount of damage that was just enough to merit another week and a half's worth of work. So we found this great house/studio that was available and rented a beautiful place at the foot of the Colorado Rockies in Loveland, Colorado. This also gave me just the right time I needed to put the finishing touches on Jesus.

In the next few months, the bronzes began to take form and I visited the foundry for one last look. I'd put those at the studio foundry under tremendous pressure with an almost unheard of deadline. There was a big debut to be held in Southern California at an architectural convention and my friend and benefactor had scheduled a spot for this sculpture to be placed that promised to be a life changer.

The excitement I felt for such an opportunity was overwhelming. Pictures flashed in my mind of architectural masterpieces like I'd seen in Europe, but with a twist of Black. I have always wanted to sculpt a public monument and have sent in countless proposals, but cities understandably want some experience under the belt. I had hoped that if these top architects and city planners were to see "The Awakening" that it would create enough of a lasting impression that it would at least give me a toenail in the door.

The foundry workers had practically worked their fingers to the bone to get the job done in time for me. We had set up a shipment and all was in order, or so I thought. As the opening of the show approached, I awaited a phone call to let me know that it arrived.

Nothing.

The sculpture never arrived. In the last few days of its assembly, a giant piece had come up missing and there was just no time to get it done for the show.

I couldn't blame anyone. It was a simple mistake. And the whole team in Colorado had bent over backwards, upside down, and inside out to get it done for me in time.

I think the most devastating blow in the whole matter was how horrible I felt in disappointing my great friend Dale. He had pulled me out of a hole a year earlier and had acted as my agent for the year to follow. He had invested a lot of money and time into the whole venture and it seemed to all come to a crashing halt in the moment I realized that I had pushed the foundry way too hard. Dale had been a godsend, but he was also a very smart businessman. He had enjoyed his philanthropic adventure in helping an artist, but his time as such was over.

Hindsight always informs me of how there really never is a good excuse to start drinking again. It didn't start right away, but as the days slipped by and I slowly darkened my days with feelings of guilt and regret, the dragon's misty breath seemed to be the only comfort inside the dark, cold and lonely corners of my mind. Over the next few years I spiraled in and out of a drunken stupor. After 11 years of living in the artist's loft at the Brew House, they would finally lose their patience with me and push me to the curb.

My daughter Angela, so aptly named, was a ray of sunshine born in the midst of the storm.

When I finally did make my move back to the west coast, my life was in a state of ruin. I had never even seen a few of the bronzes that I had done. They had gone straight from the foundry to an art facility in Ohio and I had been too caught up in my drinking to even inquire about them. So on their drive through from Pittsburgh, my brothers stopped in Ohio and paid my debt that I owed to Dale for the remainder of the bronze work and brought them west.

I had sobered up on the plane ride home. A week later, as my brothers unloaded the U-Haul, I saw some of my sculptures for the very first time. Although I had seen Jesus after he was finished many times before, he seemed a brand new work of art to me as the door of the U-Haul trailer was rolled away.

Jesus had become my truth, my light, and my freedom. This was not the traditional Jesus suffering on the cross...my dad's great idea was to see him OFF of it. Unlike many of the depictions I had grown up with, this Jesus was free...

And there we stood in the driveway, Jesus and I, off our crosses. Only I was crying. I finally understood. I was free.

I was reminded of all that time that I had worked on this sculpture and that I'd cried in its vicarious arms, just wishing someone out there would understand. I think we all get a taste of that. No one has ever really understood the fullness of who we are deep down. I LONG for this. Not in self-centered desperation, but just to share the common aspiration of lifting our spirits to soar where they so desperately belong. This can be a hard concept to explain without actually sitting down and perhaps writing it all out, and even at this, there is so much more to a story. From the outside looking in, I am pretty positive I have taken the form of a donkey that starts with an "A" many times in life. Unless you've actually lived in someone else's shoes you simply cannot comprehend what their lives, thoughts, temptations and desires are.

God has been explained as being the embodiment of love itself. There would be no room for the concepts of death, deception, judgment, fear or lies in that realm. In order to fully understand the human condition, there had to be a link. Jesus played the part of the portal as a direct link to God. This gave God the empathy needed to link the two worlds. The world in which God exists has nothing but love, life, and light. Our world, on the other hand, comes heavily laden with the fear factor. Love had to be thrown into the fire. God had to become a burnt marshmallow.

In all this, Jesus was not finished with just living through the human existence. He had to commit the ultimate sacrifice and go out with a bang. The world needed to believe in order to see. Jesus could not explain quantum theory in that day and age, even if he had, no one would have understood. So his parables, and ultimately his life, taught the existence of miracles. He suffered a horrible and torturous death for all to see. He had to prove to the world that there was life after death.

Belief in the portal is all we really need to carry us through death, destruction, and lies. I didn't have to live inside that life anymore. I was free. No more lies and hiding inside a bottle. I was off that cross and it was finished.

"Resurrection"—31" x 24" x 14" limited edition bronze

The Gateway to Creativity: The Ice Portal

There is a gateway or a portal that artists cross through to enter the world of creativity. It involves learning the basics, grasping concepts of light and color, balance and perspective in an all-encompassing manner. After just enough footwork and preparation, there is a complete change of atmosphere. It's another world. In understanding the variations we begin to see the full picture, and in seeing this broader context, we enter the world where freedom is a giant bird that swoops down to give us a new look at a horizon we have never seen before in our earthbound bodies. The first time that I translated this imaginary world into the real one, it came out in ice.

In Bruges, Belgium a European company called Inaxi was putting on one of their many ice sculpture exhibitions. These spectacular "Ice and Snow Worlds" are built inside football stadium-size tents that are temperature controlled. They had invited sculptors from around the world to create sculptures depicting the world of the imagination for this three month exhibition. I had two teammates, Mike Palumbo and the soon-to-be father of my daughter, Erik Cantine, both of whom are amazing chefs and ice sculptor extraordinaires.

We were given the awesome job of interpreting the portal to the land of the creativity. I did a sketch upon arriving and the next day we got to work on a crystal bridge held up by muses that would whisper their secrets to passersby. It was my first time carving glacier ice. Glacier ice is enormous and natural, filled with strange shards of color and mini-prisms that reflect light in ways I had never seen. For two weeks I was allowed to lose myself in this… and I did. Compared to the usual timed events I had gotten used to, this was a treat.

The Gateway to Creativity, Bruges, Belgium 2000

Artistic Drive and the Story of "Eve"

There are so many crossroads in life, so many different paths we each can take. One tiny decision leads us on a road so different than what could have happened if we had not taken a chance or a leap of faith or even decided to go against our better judgment. Sometimes it takes a rogue horse to turn a stampede in a different direction. It may not be the easy way out, but I have always been a sucker for adventure.

In the Bible, the story of Adam and Eve has love and loss as well as beginnings and endings. It's romantic, sweet, sour, and heartbreaking. It is the story of the first taste of deception. Life before Eve took the bite of the forbidden fruit was harmonious and untainted. It was not some magical apple that introduced evil into the world, it was the lie. It was the instant she decided to go against what she'd been instructed to do. In this instant fear entered the world as she knew it. There was nothing to fear inside the light of truth they had lived in before. However, in that moment, she was able to see darkness as well as light… seeing each from a new perspective of isolation. She sees the whole picture which allows the entrance of fear. Fear's children soon follow; guilt, shame, remorse and hatred…all stemming from the mother lode of deception, a gateway that let all the nasties run amuck in what could have been a perfect world forever. This blame game—that Eve was the cause—never sat well with me. I didn't feel she deserved such a boatload of scorn with one small act. But it is the truth, when we let fear enter our lives; our Garden of Eden is lost.

The decision to follow my dream as an artist was definitely not the princess cakewalk fairytale I would love to tell all the children in the world who love to draw. I loved what I did so much and had such a strange inner desire to do it, that even in the midst of hunger and poverty, the dream held me like a mother holding a baby rocking me to sleep in an oblivious manner. In these moments of deep despair, I sold my art for pennies. Paintings and drawings that took me countless hours to do provided me with not even a quarter of the minimum wage. I had nightmares about some of them, worries that the people who bought them would discard them because they felt they were worthless anyway. My heart poured into everything that I created and it was hard to ask to be paid for art that was an all-consuming passion anyway. I'm not sure whether it's a jealous reaction or just a stereotype that makes people think an artist should starve and suffer to be able to do what they love. Somehow, such notions need to be rectified. Artists as a whole deserve respect commensurate with the amount of hard work we go through as we attempt to shine some of our light into the world.

For the first time ever, instead of holding back, I am spilling this out in a highly compassionate, compelling manner in hopes that the world will give flight to the artist, instead of viewing them as "poor and starving". If we are poor and starving it'd be really cool for patrons to pay even more than we are asking for. An act of kindness such as this can do so much. To give any hard working individual a little more than they are asking for because you not only see the need and appreciate the service, but feel compelled to do so, inspires this individual to do more, work harder, spread more joy or whatever they happen to be gifting the planet with.

I love big tips. People have shown me this appreciation in the form of a large tip a few times in life and the result is overwhelming. Not only do I feed myself, my heart is touched with the feeling of being appreciated. This does not necessarily have to be in monetary form... people everywhere are craving appreciation. Just a sprinkle of this can set the world on fire inspiring lost and hopeless hearts to grab hold of dreams once again and in a roundabout way, could even start to knock out the ever existing problem of unemployment. No one wants to work hard for unappreciative bosses and patrons or next to miserable co-workers. It's easier to give up. Inspire economy. Tip JUMBO SIZE.

Appreciation is the #1 cure. It's HUGE, in every aspect of life.

In the world of art—taking a moment to really look at the persuasion behind the piece, asking the artist some questions and just having a conversation with them, you are touching the part of them that makes them thrive. In appreciating a work of art and letting this be known, you can start a wildfire of creativity. In appreciating ANYONE, you are playing the role of a doctor inside a world where there are very few of them. This sorry world is in need of many, many, many doctors of appreciation.

Most artists in this state of being are not there because they need more study time and their work is not good enough to be charging a fair price yet. That's just bull****. Fundamentals in any art form are an ongoing process, but true art in any stage is worth whatever we ourselves see in it. I'd pay a pretty handsome price for some of my four year-old's work because she tells me the story, the reason WHY she did it. I heard a quote from an artist on a radio show that a friend of mine hosts in southern California called the "Artful Undress". In this amazing and inspirational show that I hope goes on forever, my friend Kira, an incredible sculptress and writer and her artist co-host, Polina, discuss the nude's role in artwork inside today's society as well as in history. They get down to the bare necessities, the naked raw emotion of what art really is and the "why" that an artist goes through to create it. An artist that they were interviewing said to that people don't buy art, they buy the reason behind it. The "poor and starving" in the art world stems from feeling unappreciated, unaccepted and shunned from the real world. Art is looked at as just a hobby or an unnecessary toy that the world would do fine without. There have been a number of installations set up around this very theory. They've covered walls and colored the rooms with bleakness. This shed some light on what we are left with without the creative aura of art around us...but I believe it is so much bigger than that. We could not exist without the onset of creativity. We are products of the very word itself. Take it out and you'll take everything out. From the physical world we see around us in nature down to the smallest particle in the world of quantum mechanics, we ARE creativity. A new you is made every second that you exist simply by the act of observing it that way.

A painter and his or her art is just one example of many creative outlets. Just one brushstroke represents a small tap into an underground water table of creativity that stretches far beyond any imaginable state of being. Any person that decides to tap in is welcome to. And all artists can feel this deep within themselves. The way that they let it manifest itself into the three dimensional world we live in is entirely up to them. Whether through visual art, music, poetry, writing, math, science... for that matter, even a plumber can feel the creative sprinkler go off if a new idea hits him or her in the middle of a routine repair.

We enter the realm of creativity through a ring of fire, knowing full well that this portal may burn us. Some will choose not to enter. After all, the fear of being told we are not good enough and that our ideas suck is a big nasty flatulent beast that sits at the edge of this gateway discussing our horrors before we even have a chance to see if they would come true. This little turd of fear fails to reveal that these setbacks can build character and better our circumstances if only we choose to embrace them in a positive way.

When Eve took a bite of the fruit in the Garden of Eden, not only did she open a portal for fears to wash in, she opened a gateway to a higher path. Inside the entire plan—the overall view in the light of love, none is lost and all fear subsides. Light always overpowers the darkness. When we were finally able to see the dark, the light took on new value. This analogy of values represent the building blocks in the making of the creative masterpiece.

Overpowered by guilt and shame, Eve wanted to hide the truth in hopes that it would disappear. It never does. The only way out is through the light of truth. Our journey through life is finding the value of it inside the dark corners and through the revelations of the light in truth itself. We had to know the other side of the coin to fully understand the real depth of true love. It is all a part of growth. I don't think we would be such beautiful creatures without all that we go through.

In a painting I did called "Eve", the floodgates of creative juices were left wide open. Sometimes when I am in this state, I don't even realize what depth of perception is flowing through my fingers. There is always a hint of it inside the tingling sensation of discovering something new, but most often art talks to me throughout my life, beyond the creative moment. I've done paintings that have not revealed their truth until years later and still have some that have not yet "spoken" to me. In writing this book, my art is in a state of wild and happy screams and I'm finding it hard to sleep. I have never described any of the art shown in this book with the amount of depth I am now able to do right here, right now and this is flipping me out. I don't want to sleep, eat or do anything but let the words flow. It's exciting beyond belief because I'm literally learning this as I write...This writing is pouring through the portal... gates wide open... like a herd of wild horses creating a dance like no other than I have ever laid eyes on. Through it all, I'm thanking my geographical influences for the hint of West Coast tranquility and the bold East Coast candor that's transcribing each and every whisper I hear.

The fact that "Eve" is a painting that continues to teach is no surprise considering the method I used to paint the background. I have coined this methodology or technique as "God painting". I use an abstract method to spread the paint and mix the colors and after just the right amount of my end of the meddling, I let God take over. When I wake up the next day, the background is magically transformed into the most in-depth tweaks of color imaginable. No paint brush could do it... it would take eons. It is simply a method I leave to the Master.

This painting was done right after the painting called, "Uriel" which was my very first "God painting". I was in a state of flux. I knew that "Eve" was going to be displayed in the same restaurant as "Uriel". So I used the same technique to match the whole decor. But paintings are their own entities and each deserves their own story. Even the restaurant was in a state of change. Changes going on in in our lives (Erik's and mine) were swirled like the colors inside the background. No exact placement put them into being or made them into anything. In some areas there are hidden pictures or manifestations inside the paint swirls. Some I helped make... some I did not. "Eve" is experiencing a shift into the next dimension in this painting. She travels through a cold, dark ring of black fire, experiencing for the first time the gates of hell. Instead of the blame that can surround this mother of creation, there is a warm greeting and surrounding her being while she transitions in her oblivious state. It is something we all need when we are passing through darkness, and sometimes something we do not see until the pain subsides. The position that she is in is a dream state. It is exactly how I feel in the grips of creation, lifted and weightless, with a warm sensation like no other pouring through.

"Eve"—80.5"x 48"acrylic painting

Heaven and "God Painting"

Being one of many of the imperfect human beings on this planet, I would not be who I am without the hell I've gone through. For this I'm eternally grateful that I pulled an "Eve" and ate the fruit. Now I know why the light exists... and I strive to shine with it, not against it. To know this outcome in the face of the fire breathing dragon is to experience a shift in the overall perception of our existence. To act upon it is our gift back to creation.

I later used this same painting method to create a series of paintings for my church. Originally they wanted me to splash some color onto some Plexiglas for some background art to be used while a guest speaker talked about a near death experience and was going to explain what heaven looks like. I had experienced something of a glimpse of heaven myself. My church didn't know this. Nor did they know anything about my "God paintings". My good friend Brandon an extraordinary art coordinator and musician, gave me a preview of what the speaker for that day, Dean Braxton, had told him about the colors in heaven.

They are ALIVE. Nothing is dead there. Even color moves and sings and dances to the glory of life itself. It's unimaginable. We are surrounded by death here. Trees, plants, and animals corpses have formed the ground we walk on. We live in the midst of a veritable morgue. The smell of death is everywhere, but we call it dirt. I was in ecstasy immediately just in this explanation. But how could I put this kind of dimension on a two-dimensional platform? Part of this conundrum was inherently solved in using Plexiglas. The play of light and color would create an amount of depth unlike paintings on traditional opaque backgrounds. Together with the "God painting" technique, the help of a vision of my own years earlier, and an inner glow created by using the wonderful phosphorescent medium I had discovered—heaven opened its gates. Emotional bliss poured through me creating an abstract super storm of swirling colors and depths that played with light in a way that is simply not possible to convey in a photograph.

Chapter 13
LOST IN TRANSLATION

It used to upset me when my art was not seen for what I had intended. I have to admit, it still rubs me wrong when some well-meaning gentleman explains to me how sexy certain nude paintings or sculptures are. Pretty much all of my art was never made so that the world would think it's sexy. I love the element of sexiness, but it is a pale, dried-up rose petal in comparison to the all-encompassing feeling of deep inner beauty that grows like wild flowers in my garden of creativity. I long for people to see this, to somehow feel my passion and the serene beauty flowing from my fingers through the art. Sexy seems to be so face value. It only describes one facet, one surface plane of existence. And while art is obviously an outlet into this very plane... the visual, and sometimes tactile with sculpture, I long for a deeper understanding. I suppose that is why the writing happens.

At the same time, I would never want to squash someone else's translation of the art they see, mine or anyone else's. Art is an individual experience. What a viewer feels when they see a piece of art that moves them is usually a very personal matter. I love to hear people tell me what they see, and especially what they feel. Even if it is just sexy, to have brought on any reaction, the piece of art has become an instrument on which to play out the music within the viewer that longs to be heard, and it is always an honor to listen.

The art that I make now is so different from when I first started. I started with kittens, moved into skulls and dragons, sharks, and back to unicorns. When figurative painting first entered the landscape of my creative world, it was all about study. At some point it became intense study. I longed to know every fiber and every sinew that drives our anatomy into action.

The quote from Mikhail Baryshnikov has become a lifelong quest, "Fundamentals are the building blocks of fun". I studied medical books, and built the body from the skeleton on up in search of a mastery of form and will forever be in the grips of new lessons learned with each new project I take on. All along, a dance seemed to surge through my mind. It was not necessarily a sexy dance, although I'm sure it would turn some heads in that direction. It was more like the body in motion as a flame on a candle in the moonlight with a soft tropical ocean breeze, lifting it all the way into the light of the moon itself.

An Angel in the Clouds

On a beautiful moonlit night in Jamaica, I was carried away in this very fashion. I was sculpting a couple dancing in tallow for the display table in one of the island's most romantic resorts. Hundreds of couples were married there and many others were on their honeymoons. I was not. I was the only loner there.

The resort had set me up in a fabulous room overlooking the beach. I was there for one week and was treated as one of the guests, with all the perks. It was an all-inclusive resort. Everything was free - the three restaurants with fine dining, the scuba diving, the liquor. I took full advantage of all of it. But being in a couples resort in such a romantic setting all by myself was taking its toll on me. Especially because of a recent break up. Even the violin player seemed to switch to sad music when he would come and play at my table in the restaurant as he did his rounds.

After countless Cuba Libras and singing along with the happy couples at the piano bar, I'd usually stumbled to my room to sleep well and wake up for an early morning dive. Not this time. As I entered the room the sculpture that sat on my table seemed to sing to me... "Take me outside..."

So I did. Along the beautiful white sandy beach a ten foot stone wall separated a swimming pool from the crashing waves that graced the moon with a lullaby of rhythm. I placed the sculpture on the wall and sat down to work. My fingers glided across the couple in an ebb and flow that seemed to echo the sound of the waves. The light from the full moon was bright enough to almost mistake itself as daylight. The entire night rushed by in a blur. Near sunrise, a giant thundercloud had stealthily snuck up behind me. I had not noticed, and by the time tiny raindrops began to whisper a warning to take cover, I was in too deep. I could not break the flow that was rushing through me. I could literally taste the love pouring from each of the figures as their dance came to life. I longed for this. I wanted to dance and in the loneliness and solitude, I had found a partner—my clay.

Thunder clapped in an attempt to wake me from my reverie, but I was not sleeping. As the storm grew, the warm tropical rain began to pelt against my skin and bead off the wax-based tallow. We danced right into the thunderstorm and its energy penetrated straight through and into the very being of the sculpture and I could feel its heart beat. And with a loud crackle that lit the whole sky, I swore I saw a breath escape my sculpted couple's lips. Not really, but the imagination was running rampant and the thought of shouting, "IT'S ALIVE!!!" made me giggle.

As the sun made its way over the horizon, the storm clouds seemed to shrink in the majestic robes of light that were tossed across the sea. A family of cranes woke up inside the sanctity of a small fishing house just off the edge of the small bay. I watched them rattle their beaks and ruffle their feathers into alertness and then take off in the direction of the sun.

This is what art is made of… a sweet and soul warming dance that takes us far away from the worries of the moment. I was no longer alone on that island.

A gardener that happened to be passing by on his way to work offered to take a picture of me in the rising sun with the thunderous dance partner fading away into the light and promise of a new day. He didn't quite put it that way…it was more like "You want a pick-cha? Mohm?" In his thick Jamaican accent as he pointed to my camera.

Years later, as I was going through these pictures with my mom, her eyes lit up and she pointed to the clouds in the background. A silhouette of an angel filled the sky and appeared to be watching over me.

I believe angels are everywhere. They appear in the cracks between time and space, when we least expect to see them.

A Change in Direction

Translations are never lost. They are simply put through different sifters. A lifetime of experiences and circumstances lead each of us to see whatever we want to in art. I am very grateful for the translation that pours through me and equally as grateful to listen to another's.

In 2005, there was an interesting study on creativity and brain function by Alice Flaherty. It seems a lack of inhibition and an increase in dopamine are the main ingredients in the culinary concoction that makes up the delicious recipe for creativity. The frontal lobes of our brains can be seen as being responsible for generating ideas, while the temporal lobes are a filter for them. They are in charge of inhibitions and caring about what our peers think of us and our ideas. Abnormalities in the frontal lobe bringing on such things as depression or anxiety generally tend to decrease the flow of creative juice, while any dysfunction in the temporal lobes open the taps for creativity to rush through. An increase of activity in either of these lobes will outshine the other. This is why artists who don't give a rat's petootie seem to have a thread of creative genius. Together with a good shot of dopamine, which has been known to increase levels of arousal and drive while reducing latent inhibition, the creative thinker is capable of high levels of divergent thinking that is mediated by the frontal lobe. This means they can take information from anywhere and throw it in a mix to come up with a brand new concoction.

With that said, I really didn't care what the general public's concerns were about nudity. The nude figure became a vehicle for my emotions. Emotions themselves are timeless, and therefore cannot be cloaked in judgment. I felt the same to be true for the human figure. I loved shaping the curves and sinews of muscle fibers that made up the deep voluptuous flow as it so easily spilled out what my soul longed to express. In sculpture, I seemingly could push this movement to a limit only performers in Cirque du Soleil could comprehend.

But inside the two-dimensional world of painting, something got lost inside the deep study of tissue and perfection.

When Dave Smith came walking by my tent on a crisp early morning in downtown Seattle's Pioneer Square, I never expected his bright smile and charismatic handshake to be a life changer, let alone a change in the direction of my art. He was on his way to use the bathroom and was never planning to go to the art fest. So he never expected to find me either. When he stumbled across me, he handed me his card and asked if I would want to do an art show in Key West and then he was gone as quickly as he had appeared.

When I finally got around to looking Dave up on the Internet, my jaw hit the floor. Dave is an artist in his own right inside the world of promoting art. His ideas are wild and otherworldly. He is a creative genius when it comes to promoting artists and he would turn out to be my gateway into a world of painting that I was destined for from the beginning.

Many years ago, I remember being in a show where an older and much more prestigious artist was showing her work. Her name was Marie Kelly Tuiccillo. One of my best friends and fellow artists, Alison Zapata, whose heart screams for creativity just as mine does, was in the show as well. I learned this about Alison through a description from her boss at the time and my boyfriend, Erik Cantine. She was working for Erik at The Church Brew Works, a fabulous restaurant and brewery in Pittsburgh, PA who I also owe a lot to in regards to my artistic career. They still sport one of my designs on their beer label for a brew called "Thunderhop IPA". Erik was explaining that Alison was too much like me. She hated her job as a waitress and just wanted to paint. She soon became my best friend, quit working there, and to this day, lives life as a full time artist, teacher and amazing mom in my heart-throb of all cities, the "Burgh".

Alison had a special appreciation for Marie's work, and gazed at her paintings in utter amazement. I remember a tinge of judgment that entered my mind as I looked at the abstract forms strewn across her colorful paintings. I was painting every tiny detail in my work at the time. A single painting took months to accomplish. Looking back now, it was tedious and painstaking to say the least. I'll never forget the sly little eighty-something year-old grin she gave me as she watched me view her art.

"Someday you'll paint like this." she said adding, "I used to paint tight little details like you." And as she turned and shuffled away, with her smile still lighting up the air, she left one last prophecy to echo through my mind. It has never sounded so sweet as right now... "You'll learn...heh, heh....you'll learn."

It went something like that. I was young, dumb and lucky enough to be in an art show with this beautiful professional abstract painter.

At the time I took it as an insult. I actually set out to prove her wrong, painted tighter and sculpted even more detail. But then one day, I grew up. And I threw away the narcissistic mirror. Funny how things work out that way. The eighty-something year old painter with a smile as warm as Gandhi was right—in every way.

What she really said was this: "Someday you'll mature enough to let your brush go and your painting will become loose. Your thoughts will become abstract, and your heart will find freedom in all the things that you thought you knew but are finally wise enough to admit that you don't."

It had been ages since I had picked up a brush. Sculpture had become my soul's escape. But Dave Smith needed a painter. I was determined to do so to the best of my understanding and ability, hoping all the while that he would sign me.

After all, I started this game as a painter.

As you may have gathered, my drive to be an artist is, and always has been unstoppable. No matter how many times I'd heard people express their concern or negativity, there was always a part of me that held onto something bigger than that. I would force myself to explain this drive in my deepest thoughts, questioning its origin. Was it a drive for fame or money? Because the field I chose has about as much a chance at fame or money as a note in a bottle being found after it has floated across an ocean, and I knew it. Something much bigger drove my ambition. It was the same force that whispers to the wind to gallop through the labyrinth of leaves on trees and sings sweet fiery love songs to give rise to the sun on the horizon. There is no question that this drive has an intention of incredible force with the most tender of touches. Not a single thing of this world, no amount of money or power could begin to satisfy this drive inside me. As I would pour through the never-ending list of little things that seemed to make me happy, this impetus would just shake its head.

So I would ride the wind. In "full on faith" that this drive knew what it was doing and where it was going. I'm still inside this breeze and hints of direction pour through me every time I see another person who sees what I do. Every smile that crosses a child's lips when I break out the art supplies in an explosion of wistful bliss puts a twinkle in the eye of my direction.

I harnessed this drive inside the sparkling splendor of bronze and I called him "Arrow". The idea for him came to me in a funny way. We used to have a long tall hallway in our house in Ohio that led to the basement. One day a picture flashed inside my mind of how my brothers and I used to climb the walls. Using our bodies as wedges, we would inch up the wall as far as we could go before the drop became too scary. We had to work quickly too. At the sound of our parents coming, we'd stop, drop and roll, unaware of the incriminating footprints that decorated our path to a good scolding.

To have direction and know exactly what you want is an incredible attribute in today's world of choices. Our hallway adventure pose seemed to fit perfectly into a bow. An arrow that would become a man that is inside of his decision. The thought of balancing all this metal on a single fulcrum brought back the excitement of the ice carving days... only bronze would take that and run with it.

I took to the ball of clay with the same zest that inspired my every heartbeat in the world of art. "Arrow" became my drive. He sees no objects between him and his target because he is blind with faith. His piercing gaze is directed by a calling from the heart. All distractions are lost in a quiet blur of peripheral vision silenced by the soft rhythmic beats set forth by the pulse of his heart's gaze, a gaze that could pierce through any and all obstacles—more powerful than the strongest laser beam of light imaginable. He will get to where he is going, despite any cost, because he knows that is exactly what it takes. The blind faith of a single arrow...

A Story of an Arrow

A blind arrow tracing its way through the night air, suddenly stopped and found itself surrounded in the sudden rush of warmth. In all its existence it had never felt so enveloped by such a feeling. Inside this moment it felt purpose. It felt secure, and soon succumbed to the sensuous rapture... enclosed in oneness with its surroundings. A rush of sweetness swept through its very being and it began to develop a deeper sense of harmony with the place it had landed.

It soon began to drift through the fields of moments past in search of an emotional match. The arrow wished to recognize this feeling, but nothing compared. It had been cold and lonely, surrounded by others who seemed to feel the same, but had never reached out to hold it in the manner it was being held. It had felt the freshness of air rushing over its body, even the whisk of nature tickling its thin frame as it sailed from destination to destination. Previous landings were cold and brittle, scratchy and stiff...nothing like the pulsing fast paced warmth that filled its blind eyes with color. Where could this place be? Had the little arrow's cold existence finally come to its resting place? Could this be home? Maybe love... or some parallel that would take it to places....more warm places.

As images filled the little wooden frame of mind, the very layers of its skin soaked in the warmth. The arrow was filled to a point of no return. It wanted only to stay. Whatever it had landed in...wherever it was, it wanted only this. As moments grew longer, the arrow felt softer, and the pulsing that was so invigorating slowed. As if in perfect unison, the beats grew softer, and the arrow felt comfort. For the first time... comfort. Not cold, not dry... soft and wet. Slowly it drifted into a deep sleep. As the arrow slept, it dreamed.

Dreams came in unimaginable forms.... pulsating in color, slowing and sweeping landscapes of emotional bliss, and then.... a valley. Not the kind of dips the arrow was so used to feeling in every journey, but a deep, dark, cold dip. Not the kind of dry, crisp biting air it was so familiar with, but a thick, wet, cold emptiness. No darkness was darker...no cold, colder. There was nothing, no feeling, no warmth, not even the wind or the crackling loneliness that surrounded it when it was not in flight.

Suddenly, the arrow awoke only to realize that its nightmare had followed so close behind that it had jumped ahead to become its reality. It wanted out, but could do nothing. It was only an arrow, and had followed direction all its life, how could such a thing befall such a faithful servant? Was this the end? Had it come to its demise in this cold dark arena because of some wrongdoing? Had the arrow been unfaithful? Had it strayed from its course? As much as it tried it could not come to any conclusions of corruption.

Just then... a familiar warmth held its feathery tail and pulled. The arrow fought with all its might... it wanted so badly to go back to all the other arrows.... to experience another journey through wilderness without knowing its fate. The more its trusted force pulled the more the arrow wished.... but as it wished, a cold and harsh reality shoved itself into being.

The little arrow had been sitting there, so comfortable in the warmth that it had absorbed the wetness and swelled to become a part of it. As the valley in its dream came, it became heavy and soft...and could not go back to its original form. The brittle end, its last hold on a former existence....cracked.

No more rides through open air.... no more whisking through the grass, or tickling the leaves of the trees. It had become something new... something different. And yet as it sat there, it realized that its final destination was one it had been directed towards its entire life. Peace held the arrow, a kind of peace that is known only to those who experience a total acceptance, a total surrender.

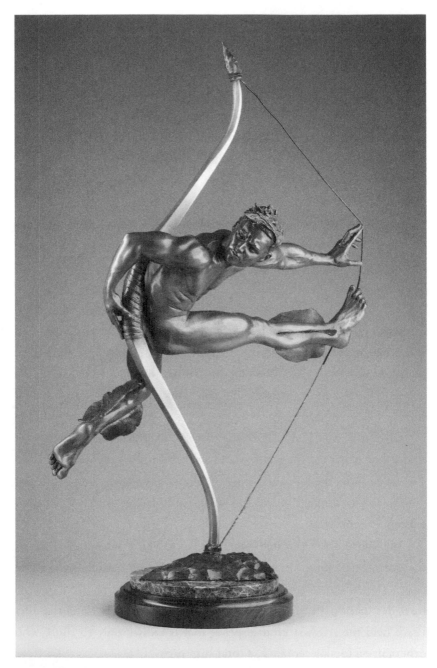

Arrow" 24"x 21"x 42" limited edition bronze

When direction is driven by the faith that holds our hearts and binds us in love, no sacrifice is too big for us to handle. The little arrows purpose was not to land in the straw stacks of target practice just as my destiny is not to adorn walls with pretty pictures. Its final destination was to feed and nourish the hand that sent it on the journey. In the moment of this realization, the arrow felt every moment of the death it was surrounded by and would soon become life again as nourishment on the table of generations to come.

The paths of artists can live forever inside the hearts of millions nourishing the hearts of lives to come for uncalculated amounts of time. It is in this that true desire cannot be matched by any other. There is and never will be anything comparable to this drive. It is the motivation that holds the desire to turn lives into masterpieces and lift every heart into a perfect symphony of love. It's the drive to inspire hope handed down with gracious hands and grateful hearts.

This is not a field occupied by artists alone. Every soul born into this life is meant to smile at the blessings it beholds inside the love he or she is surrounded by. No one thing will ever inspire the flood of dopamine pumped through our systems like a shot of true love and inspiration.

I remember growing up in the 80's and hearing that you had to step on so many heads to reach the top of the ladder of success. Possibly this ladder has been a path for some and has brought them the desires they thought they wanted. My heart feels heavy on the very thought of it. I believed people when they told me money can't buy happiness. So I sought happiness first. That road was filled with so many wildflowers that I never really went without necessity. I never starved, except when I forgot to eat because I was swept away in a momentary lapse of creative storm. I always had a roof over my head. But I've never been swimming in the laps of luxury either. It's never bothered me either way.

Little did I know that this chance meeting in the park with David Smith was about to change my direction forever in the world of art.

Dave knows what sells art. He can look at a piece and usually tell whether or not it will end up on a customer's wall. I only had the desire to make it. My only desire to sell a lot of it came in delivering a message that was hidden deep within a wall of paint or bronze that most people didn't know how to read, by no fault of their own. So unless I was able to talk to someone... one on one in a deep conversation, the art sat on a shelf. When we met, I was back at home living at my mom's house for the first time in 22 years. Although I'd traveled the world shaving a block of ice and had collectors with big names, I was displaying my twenty thousand dollar bronzes in a park next to jewelry makers and bird house crafters. I stuck out like a sore thumb. Although the jewelry and birdhouses were really quite awesome.

All my life I had struggled to meticulously depict the thoughts and emotions that spilled into the corners of my mind. Until now, I had only dabbled in the letting go, inside the freedom of abstraction where God takes hold of the brush and paints with the colors of emotional bliss. My ego wanted to control what was said but deep in the empty black corners of possibility...there lived an adventure.

Dave held the key.

But there was one last hurdle. All those years of experience gave me a bit of an ego. In the first few months of working with Dave this ego raged inside my gut with an ugly roar. From the beginning Dave told me that the artists who listen to instruction were the ones who ended up successful with his guidance. I yearned for success. Not only did it mean financial freedom no matter how big or how small the package it comes in, it also carried on its wings the possibility that these songs in my heart might be heard. So I held on to this bit of wisdom at times with both hands clenched so tight that I practically felt the teeth crackle inside the grinding motion that held my ego from denying his advice.

Slowly but surely I did let go. And as the brush strokes took hold of my hand and melted into the figures on the canvas I realized that the details didn't matter anymore. The emotions that flowed onto the canvas had to be captured like a wild panther lost in the black night. In the blink of an eye they could disappear. Instead of getting lost deep into the thought while meticulously painting the curves of a fingernail, I was getting lost in the emotion and the paint was becoming the fingernail.

My most recent work has evolved and transformed into a compilation of brush strokes, emotion and deep contemplation that hits me like poetry riding the wild and eerie green haze inside the calm eye of a tornado. A soft fluffy white halo of aura rising from a desire to lift the human spirit surrounds splashes of color from the dark cinders that once roasted my marshmallow soul.

A lifetime of listening to the music as it poured through me in color and expression can be found deep within the new Black. I don't know where this road is taking me, nor do I care. I'm in love with sharing this with everyone who takes the time to stop and listen for a moment, just as much as I love listening to them.

With every piece of art that should happen to grace your gaze with it's existence no matter what your ego screams at you in the first glance, please… remember to take a deeper look. Because whether it causes a freakish thrill, or a ghastly gasp for air this creation once started out just as you did. There is a story to learn from in the breath of every human being. Make it a pleasure to listen and inside this silent soft space that you've opened inside your heart a crystal clear diamond will soon shine rainbows of delight that reflect the appreciation of a soul yearning to be heard.

And thank you from the bottom of my heart for seeing behind the black. Here are some of my favorites in the new Black style.

"Foot in the Door" 48"x24" oil painting

Blind faith" 30"x40" oil painting

"Infinite Dreamer 24"x36" oil painting

"Wide Awake 36"x24" oil painting

"Red Crescendo" 36"x24" oil painting

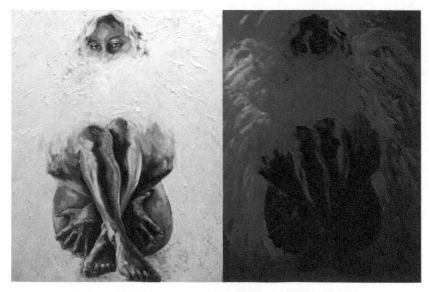

White Noise" 30"x40" oil painting and "White Noise" in the dark

"Paradidomi" 36"x36" oil painting

"Breaking Dawn"40"60" oil painting...the last two pictures are the same painting in the dark.

Blind faith" 30"x40" oil painting

"Fade to Black" 24"x36" oil painting as well as what it looks like in the dark.

Dance like nobody is watching" 30"x30" oil painting

"Guardian" 24"x36" oil painting

"Sculpted" 48"x24" oil painting

"Blue II" 48"x24" oil painting

"Manifest" 24"x36" oil painting

One Last Word on Dreams

I love dreaming. Wherever and whatever kind of dream it is, I love being inside that world. But some dreams, only a few, have been strange in otherworldly fashions. They are so intense in the most amazing way that I have held onto them for years.

One dream in particular stuck out as I rounded the corner and realized I was on the verge of ending a book that had taken me a lifetime to write. I was on a beach, in the shadows of palm trees. There was a pier off in the distance to my left and a feeling of impending doom. I looked far off into the distant sea that seemed to carry an eerie heaviness that suggested fate.

I don't remember any time between or watching a wave approach, but suddenly there was a giant muddy wall of debris filled ocean barreling into the shady trees that were once a facade of peace. I watched the faces of fear filled natives running towards me desperately searching for an instant route to safety and in a panicked realization that there was none. I'd never encountered this nationality before and I searched my memory banks in later recollection of this moment to find them with no luck.

The cold darkness of wreckage infused abyss forcefully rushed around me and lifted me from the chaos and in that moment the wave instantly turned clear. I was inside the wave surrounded by a beautiful clarity. It was more like riding a wall of beautiful blue green liquid glass than a wave of water. There was no sensation of cold or hot or even the need to breathe. It was pure bliss. The wave dropped me off on a tropical island as if it were alive. Like being softly placed by a set of giant hands filled with compassion and unconditional love.

I woke up refreshed and filled with energy. Immediately I went to my computer and wrote about it.

A few days later I learned that a giant tidal wave had devastated South Asia. The dream had been so potent that I was telling a friend about it when she interrupted me and in a delirious tone and asked if I'd even seen the news. I hadn't. I'd been lost in creativity somewhere off the face of the earth.

So I turned on the television and to my surprise, it was a gigantic wave. It was one of the deadliest natural disasters in recorded history killing over 230,000 people in fourteen countries. My heart skipped more than one beat when I saw a clip of the islanders running from a muddy wall of water. It was as if someone had filmed my dream.

This is a clip from the paragraph that I wrote that morning, "There is a tidal wave of energy starting with that dream. It rolls across the earth in a silent thunder. It will scare those who don't see it for what it is… a clean sweep for the individual soul. In it may be a fear of death… in which the soul will drown. Only faith will allow it to carry them to the new place. Why does this sound like the end of the world? It was a dream, something I had little control over. I didn't try to have control, as with lucid dreams… So now where do we go with all of this? Most of science is proving the existence of a link between matter and spirituality, or soul. It's the biggest secret and also the one that has drawn the most interest in all aspects of our lives. There is so much pointing us in this direction, and it is only a matter of time before we stop hushing the inevitable. Ride the wave without fear, without pause."

I told a few close friends about the whole incident. I hadn't experienced a premonition so huge before. I thought perhaps this was God's way of turning on the news for me, but maybe his timing was a little off.

I have recollected the dream at times in my life where there is clarity. When I have experienced a clearing of space. Writing this book has been a giant tsunami wiping me clear of any excuse not to do what is absolutely necessary and true to my expression. It wiped out any fear, that's for sure. There were excuses of not being understood and fears of being ridiculed by both the religious sectors and the non-religious ones.

I felt repressed and silenced by this, unable to dive into my artwork with full force because people did not understand it and not only was I starving from this in a lack of funds, I was alone.

Today, I will walk into my studio and enter a refreshing garden of light, allowing for every crystal to shine through me. No hindrance of fear befalls this giant leap. It's filled with a faith that a wave of clarity carries me to paradise.

EPILOGUE
Dedication, Release and a Sweet Kiss Goodbye

There is nothing like a mothers love. Mothers will go to the ends of the earth to give their children every last drop of love that rushes through their delicate hearts. We never had to fill out an application or turn in a résumé. We can confront her with our worst fears, and know that she's hanging on with us. There's no giving up. She'll pour sunshine on our rain and cry with delight over our smallest flower. She's where our roots began and will always be the life that gave us ours.

My mom is my hero. She is one of the most beautiful women I have ever met with a heart graced in forgiveness and a bottomless pit of loving care. Never once did she shed a shadow of doubt upon my sunshine. Even when my world turned black, she was there believing that I would pull through which ultimately saved my life in the end. I've watched her humbly put her life aside to give rise to others so many times in my life, and when there came a time when I needed her most...once again on the wings of an angel she soared through my dark storm and carried me to safety.

I made this sculpture before becoming a mother myself in a loving attempt to bring back the beautiful gaze that held my heart so safely in times of rejection and defeat. Realizations of why I made something subconsciously make time travel seem like something I am familiar with. This is one of the sculptures where the proof of this is evident. Mikayla was around 2 years old when I finally noticed where my model came from. It brought tears to my eyes as these things often do. I feel the strength and the love of the universe around me, and the realization that I am a part of something so beautiful and so much bigger than me.

"Tree of Life" is a representation of the envelopment of love of the biggest kind. Unconditional love. This is the knowledge that we are all a part of something bigger than ourselves that is so willing to hold us through all the growth we must endure. Every branch we unwittingly decide to climb off on as well as the roots that have formed our opinions and drive our decisions became the inspiration that relates this form of of love to a tree. Unconditional love never gives up, will never drop us and roots for the good of us all.

"Tree of life"—16"x10" x5" limited edition bronze

In saying this about the unconditional measures of a mothers love, I would never want to discount a father's love. My father has also been a rock of strength and wisdom that I was able to turn to for trusted advice on my walk through life. But I can relate to the motherly kind of love much easier, simply because of gender. This follows suit in my paintings as well. I paint and sculpt mostly women because I am one.

I owe so much of the wonders and adventure that life brings to me today to my amazing daughters, Mikayla and Angela as well as my God daughter Deanna who taught me the joy of skipping through puddles in the rain. I grew up with three brothers. I had a sister who died at birth but never had the joys of discovery that little girls take on. My soft pink fluffy unicorns and fairy princesses were run over with mini bikes, Tonka trucks and hot wheels. My brothers have become the Supermen in my life and flown to my rescue at the drop of a hat, and my daughters are like a giant puffball cloud of soft billowy love that I get to land in every time I see them. They remind me to laugh at life, giggle when necessary, and dream of faraway places in lands with castles, enchanted forests, and princes.... not frogs.

I have an adopted Grandpa that I met at my church who's taught me the joy of laughter and the importance of personalities. Lord knows he is filled to the brim with both. We are the life of the party wherever we go. His joyous and boisterous laugh will fill my heart until my dying days. No matter what wreckage life can create, inside every one of us there is the power to turn **it around. **It makes the best fertilizer for beautiful gardens and new creation to arise. And on that note, I would like to share a little poem that my daughter Mikayla and I wrote...

The Outcast

An angry cry in the middle of the night
Was how he was born, hidden from sight.

A tortured soul this whisper of wind
Out of a crack he came to ascend

At birth he broke eardrums, so small but so loud
Tormenting families and splitting up crowds

Once at the breakfast table he made the world shake
Everyone ran in fear of an earthquake

Sounding like fireworks on the fourth of July'
Noses would curl and babies would cry

No one knew what to with this chap
Everywhere he would go he was treated like crap

Sometimes he was a nuisance deciding to linger.
All knew his name, and would point their finger

At other times silent, he'd sneak into the room
Wreaking havoc, spreading cries of anger and doom.

Burning the bridges of noses became
A loss of friends and a claim to fame

But I knew him best, like a comforting pop tart
As a grateful release, my awesome friend… fart.

Laughter that lies just below the diaphragm ready to take on any moment with a sense of humor is exhilarating. While ending this book with a little comic release feels liberating and free, I have one last sculpture lingering in my mind to share. It was created in the midst of chaos, as a loving wish. I was in a toxic relationship, one that wouldn't end at the first realization of this. I'd lost any and all hopes of reviving any part of it and replaced moments of verbal abuse with dreams of freedom. This sculpture was my only peace of mind. I would spend hours sculpting away at this while he watched and thought that it was a kiss for him.

Oh it was for him alright. With every tiny detail a smile lost in its own bliss could be witnessed softly lifting the corners of my mouth in an easily mistaken ecstasy. Lost in sweet exoneration, I imagined one last kiss goodbye blown from across the room carried by angels first softly and then with lightning speed whacking his happy *** right out of my door.

May this kiss goodbye bring to you all the beautiful freedoms and new adventures that a lifetime has so graciously to offer.

MMMMMMMMMMUUUUUAAAAHHHH!!!!!

"A kiss goodbye" 12"x 13" x 10" porcelain

Acknowledgements:

Here is a list of all those listed in the book. Thank you to you all. There are a few who are not necessarily mentioned by name but without them life wouldn't be the same. I wanted to mention you here as well.

Leanne Black: most amazing mom
Jim Black: most amazing dad
Choe Chang: my step-father— who can read me better than I can
Palma Black: my step-mom—for the love and great Italian food
Tom Black: my brother who'd go to the ends of the earth for me… and has
Andy Black: my brother with a most awesome sense of humor and business partner in the new world of books
Joe Black: my brother who even moved to Pittsburgh for a few years to help me with my career
Mikayla Cantine: my amazing gymnast daughter
Angela Black: my equally amazing dreamer daughter
Deanna Webster: my God daughter
Amy Webster: Deanna's mom and my best friend
Alice Black: my grandma who gave me my artist name - C. Black
Danny Gossage: my best friend as a kid, cousin and fellow artist
Ellis Olsen: my cousin, your kindness and laughter rock
Judi Verzulli: my angel dog rescuing aunt
Erik Cantine: Mikayla's dad
Wayne Elliot: my adopted grandpa
Sharon Birch: my soul sister
Jack Richard: artist and mentor

217

Viola Rushforth: aunt who taught me oil painting
Ron Bitonio: high school art teacher
Margie Mankin: oil painting instructor in Tacoma, WA
Dale Foland: supporter of the arts and lifetime friend
Michael (Mike) Musgrave: artist and best friend
Linda Radak: Artist and friend who saw the angel with me
Mick Wood: sculptor of monsters and my inspiration to sculpt
Carolyn (Carrie) Lewis: fellow artist at Multicraft art supplies in
Akron, OH
Marie Kelly Tuiccillo: artist with words of wisdom
Joe Levak: Photographer in Akron, Ohio who landed me my first big
sculpture commission
Rich and Karen Miller: for your love and support
The Casey Family: for all of your support in my artistic career
Cindy Miller: for inspiration and artistic support
Mike Palumbo: fellow ice carver
Lucas Rendulic: for all the writing on soul mates
Alison Zapata: best friend and fellow artist
Tim and Suz Pisano: my fellow artists…You spread my wings to this day
Neal Heslop: fellow artist and inspiration
Bill McPherson: My dark angel. There can be no yin without the yang.
Thank you for the light in the dark that I needed to endure.
Tyler R. Larson: model for "Sculpted"
Bill Wessel: for putting up with me and my plants all those years
Will and Diana Harper: for your friendship and incredible film-
making talent
Robin Briejer: for your love and inspiration
Elaina Wolfe: best friend with the biggest heart
Christine Sparks: my burnt marshmallow best friend
Kira M Pandukht: Fellow artist and TRadioV host on "The Artful
Undress"

Polina Hryn: Fellow artist and TRadioV host on "The Artful Undress"

David Smith: my art publisher- thank you for all you've taught me.

Walter Smack: also my art agent-thank you for your big tips and an even bigger heart.

Don Seeley: my editor

Ana Weber: friend and fellow author

Dr. Ivan Satyavrata: leads a mission in Calcutta, India

Rupert Sheldrake: morphic resonance

Ellen DeGeneres

Colin Powell

Madame Blavatsky

Maya Angelou

Oprah Winfrey

Albrecht Durer

Morgan James Publishing: my book publisher

"What the Bleep Do We Know": movie that made me love quantum mechanics

The Brew House: Artists co-op and my roof over my head when there shouldn't have been

Life Center of Tacoma: my amazing church

Oprah Channel: for its wisdom

Publications mentioned:

"The Money Flow" by Ana Weber

"The Natural Way to Draw" by Kimon Nicolaides

"The Artists Way" by Julia Cameron

"Drinking Lightening" by Philip Rubinnov Jacobson

"Multifaceted and Fabulous" by Ronda Fisher

Other characters:

Dragons: alcohol and other addictions

Big bad wolves: greedy individuals
Fairies: angels
Frogs: God's reminders to love more and hate less
Burnt Marshmallows: all the soft warm hearted souls who've been
burnt

About the Author

Colleen Black is a world-renowned artist represented by various galleries throughout the United States as well as some that are in a very literal sense "overseas". Various Caribbean and International cruise lines are some of Colleen's most recent purveyors of her artistic endeavors. She studied painting in Italy at The Florence School of Art and gives great credit to her mentor Jack Richard, a very well-known artist of soul and spirit in Cuyahoga Falls, Ohio. Her commissions include completing a limited edition sculpture and oil painting for General Colin Powell as well as seven Congressional Medal of Honor recipients.

In addition to finishing her new book and promises of others that are already in the works, Ms. Black is currently working on a series of paintings and monumental bronzes, as well as a line of one-of-a-kind women's handbags and accessories called "C. Black Pursenalities". Presently she lives in Puyallup, Washington with her two daughters and is continually exploring the inner universe, the soul's link with quantum mechanics, enlightenment, and the questions that serve to drive us into a new understanding of our innate creativity.

"My goals have always been to touch some deeper side of people's reality... to plant a seed. People can get a sense of helplessness in the face of tragedy. My hope is that this work may just open a door, or even a window, and shed some light on a new direction... a new movement... a new personal renaissance. There is a deeper side of existence and its discovery is profoundly more beautiful than mere surface qualities. Look beyond what you see, and have faith that there is something more. Mustard seeds really do have the ability to move mountains."

– C. Black

CPSIA information can be obtained at www.ICGtesting.com
Printed in the USA
BVOW10s2033201014

371608BV00003B/3/P